create your own

tabletop

fountains

paris mannion

NORTH LIGHT BOOKS
Cincinnati, Ohio
www.nlbooks.com

dedication

This book is dedicated to fountain enthusiasts everywhere.

a note about safety

The author and publisher disclaim any liability for damages or injury resulting from the use of this information.

photo credits:

Photographs on pages 31 and 41 are copyright March 1999 by Tanya Inman.

05 04 03 02 01   5 4 3 2 1

Library of Congress Cataloging-in-Publication Data

Mannion, Paris
  Create you own tabletop fountains / by Paris Mannion
    p. cm.
  Includes index.
  ISBN 1-58180-103-3 (pbk. : alk. paper)
  1. Tabletop fountains. I. Title

TT899.74 .M36   2001
745.593—dc21   00-060080
                                                CIP

Editor: Nicole R. Klungle and Maggie Moschell
Designer: Amber Traven
Production coordinator: Sara Dumford
Production artist: Ben Rucker
Photographer: Christine Polomsky
Beauty Shot Photographer: Al Parrish
Beauty Shot Stylist: Jan Nickum

about the author

Paris Mannion, LCSW (Licensed Clinical Social Worker) and Certified Professional Coach, has been building fountains since 1995. After experimenting with different crafts, she discovered many art forms that lend themselves to fountain construction. Working with stained glass, clay, copper, bamboo, gourds, slate, shells and ceramic tile, she became familiar with many tools never used in her psychotherapy practice. With two drill presses, a band saw, a rotary tool, a glass cutter as well an assortment of pumps, lights, tubing and bowls and finally a workshop, Paris likes working with her hands.

"Drilling holes in slate and rainbow rock is one of my favorite things to do. It's very therapeutic and the results make terrific fountains!" she explains. As a professional coach helping people get clear on their values, set goals, make plans and take action, Paris encourages her clients to build personal fountains to balance hard work with creative play. The state or condition of the fountain (well tended or neglected, for instance) seems to reflect the person's mental or emotional condition. Paris offers a unique opportunity for people to use their hands to effect change in their surroundings, spur personal transformation and create a beautiful gift. Because each fountain builder arranges the fountain and selects the finishing touches, no two are the same. Crafting a fountain is a reminder of our connection with nature as well as a connection to an inner self. Paris is a featured workshop leader at the Learning Annex in San Diego, guiding fountain enthusiasts as they craft their personal fountains.

acknowledgements

My thanks to Glenn Harrison at Fountain Pumps, Inc., in Downey, CA, for the loan of his fountains for the gallery and construction advice for several fountains. Elaine Nobriga, a fountain builder in Ignacio, CO, also contributed a feather rock fountain as well as support and encouragement. Kaye Stinger and Janet Beyries at Paint and Clay in La Costa, CA, graciously shared tips on tinting and spreading grout for the stained glass mosaic. Luba Semanisin, from Rancho Bernardo, CA, painted flowers on rocks following Lin Wellford's book and donated her creations to our fountain efforts.

Tanya Inman, multitalented photographer, desktop publisher and graphic artist in Sunnyvale, CA, took the wonderful pictures of European fountains. The fountain fans participating in the tabletop fountain discussion group at egroups.com were a big help with copper cutting and soldering tips. Carol Lang, gourd artist in Carlsbad, CA, taught our class to cut and woodburn those pumpkinlike vegetables. Sammie Crawford, the "Fairy Gourdmother™," contributed gourds for the gourd fountain project. Doug Green, master gardener in Canada, and Joy Somes, Pond Lady in Florida, shared ideas on water plants. Gloria Hoover, rock hound, shared her insight into creating rolling spheres. Susan Pickelsimer, fountain teacher in San Francisco, gave me the idea for the basket fountain and donated a fountain cushion. Anne Geldert, fountain maker in Ramona, CA, shared tips on the vertical pipes bamboo fountain during a fountain building TV show.

table of contents

introduction

When I saw my first tabletop fountain in 1995, I had no idea how popular they would become or how gripped by their creation I would be. I was attending a Feng Shui lecture at a book and gift store in Los Altos, California. On my way to a seat I walked past a small, round, black bubbling fountain. I didn't know exactly what I was looking at, but the fountain seemed familiar. During the talk, the presenter rattled off some associations we have between water and money, such as cash flow, liquid assets, and laundered money. Her point was that Feng Shui (pronounced fung schway, meaning "wind-water" in Chinese) can influence prosperity, wealth, energy and harmony in our home and work environments, and that indoor fountains are inexpensive and effective Feng Shui tools.

Put off by the eighty-five dollar price tag, I thought that night about how I could make one. A friend suggested a hardware store for a submersible pump and a lapidary store for some nice-looking rocks. Well, I spent a lot more than eighty-five dollars on each of several fountains I put together. But what fun! A few years previously I had studied fifteenth-century fountain pictures as symbols of change and washing off of the old to make way for the emergence of something new. And now here was a new craft and an elegant new way to reconnect with nature by bringing water sounds indoors.

Fountains in the home help in many ways. They clean the air by pulling in particles, lint and dust, and also humidify dry air in rooms heated by forced air in winter. Plants grow more lushly around fountains, pets are calmer near them and people relax to the gentle, soothing water sounds.

When water droplets are sheared, negative ions are released, the kind that promote better mood, sleep and concentration. Spirits lift when you see a visually pleasing sight in a living or sleeping space. I've seen fountains in some creative places in homes, such as on a staircase landing, on a pedestal in the living room, tucked in a bookcase and masquerading as a lampshade in the guest room.

At work, fountains facilitate clear thinking, better concentration, improved communication. They provide a white noise to mask machine sounds and offer a calming visual that soothes jagged tempers. A desktop fountain may even defuse violent tempers at work. Water "speaks" in a murmur as it tumbles, making a fountain a "poem in stone."

As I began leading fountain-building classes, I was impressed with the infinite variety of fountain compositions. Each unique creation reflected the owner's imagination and style. Are you ready to unleash your inner fountain artist? Let's get started!

getting started

This section will tell you about the supplies and materials you will need for fountain building. Each project lists the supplies to purchase.

The tools for creating your tabletop fountain can be found at most hardware stores.

tools

Picture of tools, starting upper left, clockwise:

1 terra-cotta sealant to keep water from seeping out of clay pots, with brush
2 spray bottle of water to keep the dust down while drilling and to see what rocks will look like wet
3 metal pipe-cutting tool
4 small screwdrivers, tweezers in yellow case, to screw the cutting wheels onto the rotary tool when cutting metal tubes
5 variable-speed electric drill with case of drill bits
6 blue and white tube of epoxy putty (to fill holes), small tube of Goop (underwater adhesive)
7 copper scrubber to clean gourds
8 soldering iron with paste flux and brush
9 rotary tool with ceramic drilling bit

10 white putty knife for spreading grout on mosaic fountain
11 screwdriver and Phillip's head screwdriver for tightening nuts on Watering Can fountain
12 craft scissors for cutting sheet of copper
13 rasp for filing drilled holes
14 ruler
15 wire cutter to cut copper wire
16 needle nose pliers for shaping wire
17 meat baster to suction water out of fountain for cleaning or to remove excess water
18 scratch awl and wooden head awl to puncture holes in copper pipe
19 E6000 clear underwater glue to glue glass tiles to glass bowl in Glass Mosaic fountain

20 latex gloves to wear when working with adhesives
21 hammer to pound awl into copper pipe
22 wood stain for gourd (optional)
23 dust mask

Center of picture:
24 can opener to open the wood stain can
25 craft knife with sharp blade to cut rigid tubing
26 wrench to tighten the nuts and bolts in the Watering Can fountain
27 hacksaw to cut bamboo, river cane and rigid plastic tubing
28 scissors

fountain pumps

A wide variety of small, submersible electrical pumps are available today for your fountain-building pleasure. Check garden centers, hardware stores, aquarium stores and the Internet for indoor fountain pumps. The most popular pumps are about 2" (5.1cm) square. Inside the cover is the propeller, which rotates around a metal or ceramic shaft. The spout from which the water emerges is on top.

Most have a screened intake valve in the front or on the side. Some have the intake valve on the bottom and can be used in very shallow bowls. Water is pulled in through the intake valve, spun forward by the propeller, and forced out the pump spout on top. The propeller rotates around a ceramic or metal shaft that is sealed off from the electric motor. New on the market are battery-operated pumps that go for two to three days before the four D batteries run out of juice. (See Resources page 126.)

Pumps will also have something to keep them from sliding about the bowls. Look for three or four little suction cup feet that anchor the pump securely to the bottom of the bowl. Some models have a rubber O ring or rubber strips to keep them in place.

Pumps come with thin cords and two-prong plugs (indoor use only) and with thick cords and three-prong (grounded) plugs (indoor or outdoor use). For safety, create a dew loop where the cord dips lower than the outlet before rising to be plugged in. This way any water that may splash out of the bowl along the cord will drip off before the cord reaches the plug.

Look for pumps that have a water flow regulator so you can adjust the water pressure from a trickle to a gusher. The pressure is controlled by a water flow regulator bar, which can be raised or lowered. The maximum gallons per hour of most tabletop fountain pumps is 70 to 90 gph (276 to 342 liters per hour).

This is a fountain pump.

This shows the feet, the propeller and the spout.

The dew loop will prevent water from shorting out your electrical outlet.

flexible plastic tubing

Flexible vinyl plastic tubing or hose is used to elevate the water or aim it in a different direction. There is a size to fit every pump spout; the most common diameter tubing is ⅝" (16mm) outer diameter (o.d.) with ½" (10mm) inner diameter (i.d.). Tubing can also be used to increase or decrease the water pressure. If you want a softer water flow at the top of your fountain, you would look for tubing that fits outside the ⅝" o.d. If you want more of a jet effect, look for tubing that fits inside the ½" i.d. Then just cut off an inch or so of the new tubing with a pair of scissors and slide it outside or inside your ⅝" piece. Look for plastic tubing in aquarium, hardware, and pool and pond supply stores.

A Y-attachment is a clear plastic adapter that fits into the tubing to direct the water in two directions. It's used on page 36.

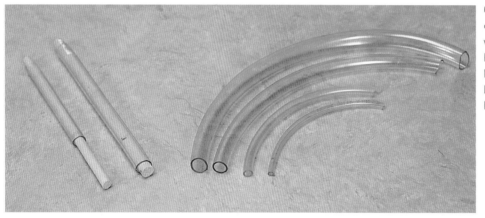

Common sizes of vinyl tubing include (right side of photo, starting with the largest): ⅝" i.d. by ¾" o.d. (16 x 19mm); ½" i.d. by ⅝" o.d. (12 x 16mm); ⅜" i.d. by ½" o.d. (10 x 12mm); and ¼" i.d. by ⅜" o.d. (6 x 10mm).

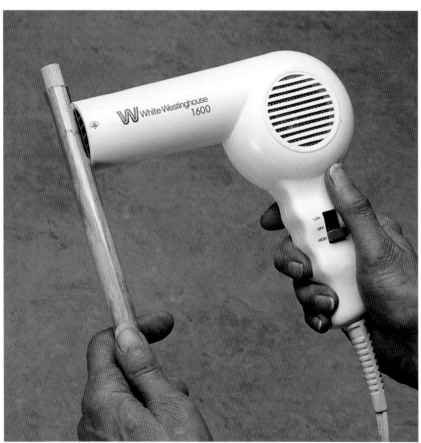

Flexible tubing generally comes in coils and retains the curve when you cut off a piece, like the tubing on the right. You can straighten a length of tubing by sliding a wooden dowel through the tubing and immersing it in boiling water for about ten seconds (see photo above). Let it cool and slide it off the dowel by pushing from one end and pulling from the other. The tubing will be straight. Another way to straighten tubing, shown at left, is to slide a wooden dowel through the tubing and run a hair dryer over it for about eight minutes. Let the tubing cool on the dowel. When you slide it off, the tubing will be straight.

cutting tubing

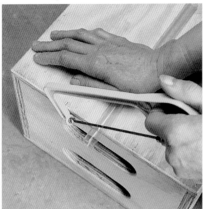 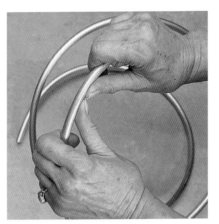

For the Magic fountain and Tiered Clay Pot projects, you will use stiff plastic tubing from an aquarium store. Use a small handsaw to cut this tubing because it will crack and splinter if crushed with scissors.

Like plastic tubing, copper tubing comes in various diameters. For the Copper Leaf fountain and for the stand of the Gourd fountain, I used a ⅜" (10mm) o.d. coil of refrigerator tubing from the hardware store.

Cut copper tubing with a metal-cutting tool (pictured on page 60) that acts like a vice with a sharp wheel that cuts the metal as you turn the tool. For best results tape over the area to be cut so the wheel blade will grip the tape first and not slide up and down the pipe.

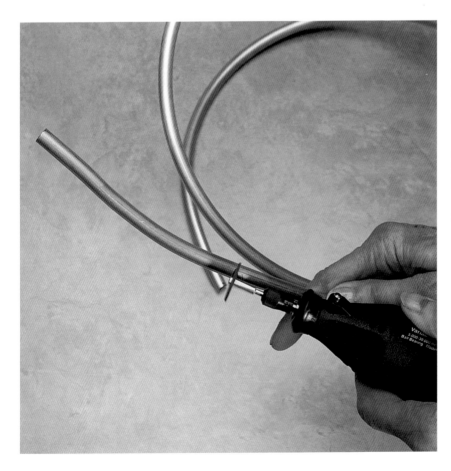

You can also cut copper pipe using a rotary tool with a wheel specially designed for this purpose. Because the wheel is brittle, you'll have better results and less breaking of the wheel if you thread two wheels on the head of the tool. Hold the tool steady and slowly feed the copper into the spinning wheel edges.

Toward the end of the cut, the copper pipe may fall away with just a little bit of metal holding the two pieces together. Just bend one end back and forth until the break is complete. Don't use tin snips to cut copper pipe or the round edges will be flattened together.

There are several choices of PVC collars in different heights at hardware stores (first collar in the photo). Elevate the collar by gluing three bottle caps to the bottom edge. The third collar shows a bottomless plastic pot with notches cut into the bottom.

This is how the pump fits inside a collar. The notches allow the water to enter and the cord to exit.

collars

PVC collars or platforms are used to shield the pump from heavy objects sitting on its back. Pumps are sturdy enough to bear weight, but the spout sticks up in front on most pumps and can be an unstable surface. For instance, the pump may tip over if a heavy, drilled stone is placed over the spout.

There are several choices of PVC collars in different lengths at hardware stores. Look for sections from 2" to 4" (5.1 to 10.2cm) long. PVC drainage pipe is less expensive than PVC plumbing pipe.

Saw notches in the PVC collar to allow water to enter the intake valve freely and the cord to exit the collar easily. Some pumps have the cord fairly high up, so that will determine how high your notches need to be. Use a hacksaw, electric miter saw, table saw or small, inexpensive two-blade saw. This small saw for metal, plastic or wood is often located on racks near the checkout stands of hardware stores. Make two cuts about ½" (12mm) apart, and wiggle the plastic back and forth until it breaks or angle the second cut so it meets the first in a V. Make three or four notches.

You can also saw the bottom off a plastic flowerpot or cottage cheese container, invert it and use it as a collar. Elevate the collar by gluing three plastic bottle caps to the bottom edge so the water can easily get to the pump.

Water is the source of life and the focus of your tabletop fountain.

water

Some people use distilled water in their fountains to minimize white mineral deposits. However, if the fountain is in direct sunlight, it will be more vulnerable to algae growth with distilled water. Also, distilled water can cause shells to lose lime to the water.

Most people fill their fountains with tap water. The slight chlorine in tap water helps keep down algae growth as do fountain products such as Fountec and Fountain Block. If your water is hard and mineral deposits form white scale, soak the pump, stones and bowl in vinegar and water (1:1) overnight. Mineral deposits can also be removed with a paste of cream of tartar and water. There are other fountain products to reduce scale, such as Protec. (See Resources page 126.)

water sounds

You will want to control the sound of the water in your fountain. If the sound of the water is too loud, you can adjust the pump's water flow regulator to reduce the water flow. You can also increase the amount of water in the bowl to mute the sound. If the sound isn't loud enough, try decreasing the amount of water in the bowl. Remember to leave enough water to prevent damaging your pump.

Another way to alter the sound is to lean a concave stone or shell over the water source to diffuse the water. Or interrupt the fall of water by putting stones or shells in its path.

water splash

To minimize water splash and furniture or floor damage, keep rocks away from the edge of the bowl. Water that hits rocks that touch the bowl's rim will splash out. You can also angle rocks inward so if water splashes onto the rocks, it will flow back into the bowl. Another way to control splash is to reduce the water pressure using the regulator bar on the pump

The way you design your fountain affects the amount of splash. Use a "sounding stone" so water hits the stone and not the water pool below, to reduce splash. Another approach is to reduce the height of the fountain inside the bowl. That is, don't build the fountain up too high.

However, if you have your heart set on a tall, loud, splashy fountain, you can put it on a mat or rug to protect the floor or table from the water.

water levels

Keep the water level well above the pump intake valve for smooth flow. If the water level falls low, you will hear a distinctive gasping, struggling sound from the motor.

Don't run the pump out of water or the motor will burn out. Check the water level daily for the first three or four days to determine the rate of evaporation. Just as your houseplants need watering, your fountain will need water every so often. You will also notice that the humidity of your house at various times of the year affects how frequently you must add water.

Here are some containers for fountains. Your fountain bowl should be at least 3" (7.6cm) deep to well cover the intake valve and can be from 6" to 20" (15.2 to 50.8cm) wide. Pumps with bottom intake can operate in bowls 1½" (3.8cm) deep.

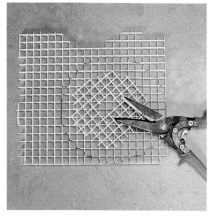

A deep container can be fitted with a plastic tray insert so fewer rocks are needed and your fountain will be easier to lift. Cut a fluorescent light cover with ½" (13mm) grid (from the hardware store) with heavy-duty craft scissors and place the circle inside the bowl's rim. Enlarge the grid for the pump spout and tubing to come up. Then put your stones and decorative items on top of the grid. Or use the lid of a large cottage cheese container, cutting an X for the spout and tubing to fit through.

This gourd was given a copper patina following these steps:
• Clean the gourd inside and out.
• Paint on the Chemtek copper paint and let dry.
• Pour on more copper paint for the dripping effect, then spray with the Chemtek green patina.
• Let it oxidize and dry.
• Spray with several coats of polyurethane spray.

This shows the Chemtek kit that has everything needed to create a copper patina on containers such as gourds and metal bowls.

containers

Bowls made of ceramic, seamless metal, glass or plastic make great fountain containers. You can also use a container of clay or wood if you waterseal it or line it with plastic. Check your cupboard for a pasta or serving dish, punch bowl, casserole dish or fruit bowl if you're in a hurry to make a fountain.

Finding suitable containers for your fountain can be fun. Check out flea markets, import stores, housewares catalogs, thrift stores, garden centers, department and discount stores (housewares department) for something that suits your fancy. Or take a pottery class and fashion your own hand-built or wheel-thrown container.

You can customize your ceramic, glass or metal container by painting it with acrylic paints. The Desert Oasis fountain (page 120) uses a stainless steel mixing bowl sprayed with primer and a sand-textured paint. Metallic paints will add a copper or brass patina to any material. Protect the paint with three to four coats of polyurethane spray.

Even something unusual, such as a basket, can be used for a fountain if you put a plastic or glass insert in it first. You'll know you're "hooked" on fountain making when you look at nearly every container and think, *I could make a fountain out of that!*

The clay pot hole is filled with epoxy putty, a two-part putty that comes in a stick and hardens in twenty-four hours or less. Break off a piece and mush it together so the two parts blend. Then lay it over the hole you want to cover. If the material surface is dirty, clean it with denatured alcohol first. If used in an outdoor fountain, coat the putty with silicone sealant when dry to protect it.

sealing

clay

Unglazed clay containers need to be watersealed or water will seep through the clay and puddle under your fountain. For waterproofing clay pots, a hardware store will have several products:

- terra-cotta sealants in spray or liquid
- small containers of concrete and masonry sealant
- spray or liquid polyurethane
- acrylic sealants in spray or liquid
- latex-based sealant, such as Drylok (goes on like paint, cleans up with water)

metal

Some attractive metal containers from craft stores have legs, but the screws attaching the legs penetrate the bowl. Fortunately, you can seal against water leaking with several products. Lay a strip of one of these materials from hardware or craft stores along the crack or break in the metal:

- silicone caulk for kitchen or bath
- aquarium sealant
- Mr. Sticky's Underwater Glue
- E6000, a clear glue from craft and hardware stores that dries in twenty-four hours.
- epoxy putty

These products are also used to seal drainage holes on gardening pots or bonsai bowls that you may like for fountain containers. Just put some electrical tape on the back of the hole, turn the container over and fill the hole with your glue, sealant or caulk. Pull the tape off when the sealant has hardened.

slate and wood

Some fountains incorporate slate pieces. If your slate has unusual tinges of red or green, you may want to preserve the colors by sealing the slate. Concrete sealant or polyurethane will do the trick.

Wood bowls also need to be watersealed (or fitted with a plastic liner) to prevent warping and cracking. To waterproof wood, you also have several choices from the hardware store:

- fiberglass and resin (smelly, expensive)
- plastic laminate
- marine varnish (sticky, not always available)
- a plastic liner tacked or stapled above the water line
- a waterproof container placed inside the wooden bowl or box on which you build your fountain

gluing

You can glue your fountain pieces together so they don't move around, but be sure you can remove the pump to clean it four times a year. Wear disposable latex gloves when working with these chemicals from the hardware store:

- E6000
- epoxy putty
- silicone bathtub caulk can be used as glue in a pinch
- Mr. Sticky's Underwater Glue adheres to ceramic, metal, glass, plastic, rubber, styrofoam, wood and other materials

Shells such as conch and abalone have natural spouts for water flow. Adjust the plastic tubing so it releases water into the shell just where the shell lip starts to spread out. The water will flow forward out the narrow end of the conch or out the side holes of the abalone, with no drilling needed.

Z-lite rocks with sandblasted holes and driftwood make great fountainheads.

fountainheads

A fountainhead is an item to put on top of the pump spout to hide the water source. Since a fountainhead needs a hole for the water to come through, look for items that already have holes or items that can be drilled.

The following are some fountainhead materials:

rocks

- Rocks with natural holes, such as lava rock (from a pet or aquarium store), tan-colored tufa rock or variegated rainbow rocks. Smooth, gray "holey stones" from the beach have tunnels and holes created by urchins and other sea creatures. Lower the water flow of your pump if the small hole increases the water pressure. Z-lite rocks have sandblasted holes and can be found in aquarium stores. (See Resources for more information.)
- A geode slice with tiny crystals lining the center hole. This makes a nice waterfall when placed horizontally over the spout.

seashells

- Sea urchins and Mexican sand dollars have natural holes that balance easily over a pump spout.

hardware store items

- A copper elbow from the plumbing department, which sends water out in a curve. A copper T directs water in two directions.
- Drilled slate. A 12" (30.5cm) square slate tile is easy to break and drill. (See Drilling page 21)
- A terra-cotta clay pot, set on its side so water flows out over the rim. Drill a ⅜" (10mm) hole on the side or bottom with an electric drill and ceramic tile bit (or rotary tool with ceramic bit). Fit the pot over the pump spout.

craft store items

- A large wooden or ceramic beads is nice for a small desktop fountain as the water just goes up and comes down over the bead.

Clockwise from left, accents are bleached cactus spine resting on some driftwood, a one-piece ceramic trio of vases, a carved stone, a butterfly, a shell, luster gems and a flower painted on a rock. In the center are a piece of blue abalone shell and a natural sponge.

accents

Adding accents to your fountain is the easiest way to personalize it. There are accents to suit every taste and decor. To stimulate your imagination, here are some popular fountain decorations.

plant cuttings

For a natural touch, spider plant, ivy, bamboo shoots or any plant that roots in water can be slipped between rocks. Remove the cuttings and add new ones when the roots are well developed. Air plants, on the other hand, need to keep their roots out of water.

flowers

Silk or live flowers give color to a fountain scene. Flowers that grow near water, such as irises, can be stuck on pin frogs or in florists foam and placed in the fountain. Put a geranium or daisy among the rocks or float a rose or gardenia on the water.

fire

A tea candle on a flat rock, in a glass cup or on a small metal stand, or a floating candle in the pool adds an unusual contrast of opposites, fire and water. An oil lamp is also attractive.

animal figures

A stone carved or ceramic frog, fish or turtle contributes to the outdoor pond image; green patina dragonflies, butterflies, salamanders and totems are also popular.

driftwood

To keep driftwood in good shape, keep it out of water. If you do want it in your fountain water, remove it every few months and let it dry out or it will shred. Glue an air plant on driftwood with Liquid Nails, fingernail polish or a glue gun.

birds

Little feathered birds from craft stores can be attached to driftwood "trees" to grace the fountain garden. Birds are also made of ceramic, glass, wood and metal.

statues

Figurines of Buddha, Kwan Yin, dragons, fairies, mermaids and kachina dolls are often displayed in fountains. In addition to import stores, also check aquarium supplies for statues that go in fish tanks.

crystals and semiprecious stones

Rose quartz, amethyst and fluorite sparkle in the sun and glow with an underwater light. Chunks of these crystals also come carved with a depression for a tea candle. For color, add polished semiprecious stones such as tiger's eye, sodalite, citrine and malachite.

mirror

Place a mirror behind a candle or in front of a pump spout, so the water flows over the mirror. From a Feng Shui perspective, a mirror behind a fountain will expand its energy.

glass

Luster gems are small flattened marbles that add touches of sparkling color. Look for bags of them in craft or garden stores.

rocks and stones

Rocks and stones can be found outdoors everywhere. Garden and craft stores sell bags of polished river stones. Check the Yellow Pages for companies that sell colored pebbles and aqua cove, small pale blue and green stones from the Philippines.

plants

When the air or energy in a room seems stale or too dry or the sunlight is too harsh, you can apply a Feng Shui cure. As living objects, plants are one of the nine cures. Added to the fountain's running water (another Feng Shui cure), they amplify the positive energy, or *chi,* and help balance the room's energy. Live plants also remind us of our connection to nature.

dwarf water plants

If your fountain will have six hours of sunlight a day, try these additions from February through September. (Water plants go dormant in the winter.) Check with the nursery on growing and maintenance conditions:
- pampas grass
- fern
- palm
- sweet flag
- water lettuce matures at 4" (10.2cm) span
- duckweed
- water hyacinth (will last about three months indoors)

air plants

These light gray-green flowering air plants like warm, humid conditions and dry roots. They can be nestled above the water line among the fountain stones or glued onto rocks, shells and driftwood to blend in with the fountain. To glue the air plants on rocks, use Liquid Nails or a glue gun. Some varieties that work well are air plants from Mexico, Guatemala and Honduras. Air plants are also known as bromeliads or tillandsias and are available at garden centers, nurseries and on the Internet.

plant cuttings

Green plant cuttings that root in water can be placed in the fountain. Plant them in dirt after roots develop to about 1" (2.5cm). Meanwhile siphon water out regularly with a meat baster to keep plant debris to a minimum. Hide the pump cord by placing these cuttings around it:
- spider plant
- Swedish ivy
- philodendron
- pothos

moss

- Transplant moss from the forest by simply peeling a delicious moss chunk off its home area and draping it over a tufa rock, chunk of clay pot or granite stone. Moss likes (1) damp, (2) shade, (3) acidic conditions for the most part and (4) regular and constant temperatures. Provide these things and you can grow moss, says Doug Green, gardening magician in Canada.
- Find pale green moss in some florist shops.
- At a landscape yard, look for a palm-sized piece of mossback sandstone. Gray lichen rests dormant on the stone, just waiting for water to spring it into green life in your fountain.

Plants, rocks and water combine beautifully in nature and in your fountain.

maintenance

- Check water level daily for the first week to note amount of evaporation. You will be surprised at how much water is lost to air as the fountain humidifies your environment.

- Mist air plants two or three times a week with soft or bottled water. Use a diluted fertilizer in summer months.

- Keep water level as full as possible for best pump operation. The pump motor functions best when it has plenty of clean fluid circulating, just as your car motor needs oil.

- Add a few drops of bleach to the water to inhibit algae growth if this is a problem. Fountains in direct sunlight will develop algae quicker than if they are in the shade. After adding two drops, wait fifteen minutes and sniff the water. If you can smell the bleach, you are OK. If you can't, add another two drops.

- Siphon water out after two weeks with a turkey baster to check sediment level. Dust, hair and lint will collect in the bottom of the bowl, pulled from the air by moving water. Refill with clean tap water.

- When the cord gets slimy, the rocks feel slippery or you see visible sediment, prepare to take the whole fountain to the sink for complete cleaning and fountain rebuilding. Regular cleaning about every three months preserves the life of the fountain pump. Debris around the intake valve and propeller can slow and strain the motor.

- Remove top accents such as shells, crystals and plant cuttings, and rinse separately. Carry the fountain bowl to the sink and remove the remaining rocks and pump. If you are using a piece of wood in your fountain, remove it and let it dry out if it starts to shred.

- Clean the pump by wiggling off the front part that covers the propeller. When in doubt, follow manufacturer's instructions. Pull the propeller out and remove hair, lint, etc., rinsing thoroughly. Carefully clean residue from other visible parts of the pump, including the bottom.

- Remove hard water deposits with vinegar, Lime-A-Way or cream of tartar (from the grocery's baking section). Lime-A-Way will dissolve shells (which are made of lime); if using this product, make sure to rinse the bowl well after cleaning.

- Reassemble your fountain. Perhaps choose a different bowl and accents or put your fountain in a different location to enhance the *chi* in the new area. Enjoy!

A turkey baster is a no-mess way to remove old water from your fountain. It's amazing how much stuff ends up in the bottom of the bowl and on the pump!

shaping slate

Landscape yards carry handsome black patio slate, often very large pieces. With a little strength and courage you can break them into manageable sizes. This demonstration uses thin slate from the flooring department at Home Depot. This chain and other hardware and tile stores carry 12" (30.5cm) square slate tiles from India at less than two dollars each. The main advantages of this slate are the following:

• It is easy to drill because it is not as dense as some slate from the landscape yard.

• The edges chip off easily with a hammer and can be tapped into the shape you want.

• The ½" (13mm) tile can be drilled through in under ten minutes.

1 You can break slate against two cinder blocks or a street curb. Wear gloves and eye protection because you can never predict when a piece of slate will fly up toward your face. Position the slate so the grain is horizontal. Whack the tile firmly at a 45° angle. If the angle and force are right, the tile will break in two.

2 Repeat this with the two halves until you have four pieces about 3" (7.6cm) square. You can also hammer the piece in two with a sharp, firm stroke to the slate overhang close to the cinder block. This works best for smaller pieces.

3 You can rough up the square cut lines to give the slate a more natural, irregular look by chipping it with a hammer.

4 To shape the edge, slide about ½" (13mm) of the slate over the edge of the cinder block. Press down firmly with the heel of your hand to stabilize the piece. Using a short grip on the hammer, tap away the edge of the slate, moving along the edge.

drilling slate, tile or rocks

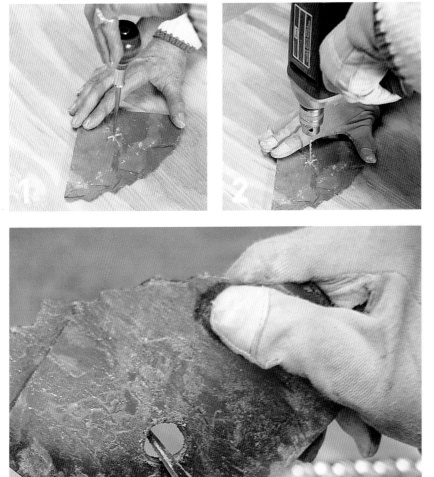

1 Mark an X where you want the hole to be drilled. Twist an awl or ice pick into the center of the X.

2 If the bit slides on the surface, put an X of masking tape where the hole will be. Set the slate piece on plywood. Using a small-diameter bit, say ¹⁄₁₆" (2mm), in a five-speed electric drill (set on medium speed), drill into the little spot dug out by the awl, all the way through. This pilot hole will guide the larger bit in moving more easily through the stone. Change the drill bit to ⅝" (16mm), the size of the tubing.

3 Remember to keep the drill vertical. If your slate is thicker than ½" (13mm), stop a few times to spray the hole with water. This keeps the bit cool and reduces dust. You will notice a different, more intense buzz as the bit begins to penetrate out the other side. Just keep going until you hit wood and the hole is drilled all the way through.

4 If the bit did not cut the slate cleanly and the hole is not as round or wide as you need, just scrape away the excess with the edge of a knife or scissors. These directions can also be used to drill ceramic tile.

safety precautions:
- Protect eyes.
- Protect hands.
- Clamp the slate to prevent it from spinning if the bit catches when penetrating it.
- Let the drill do the work rather than force the drill down into the stone.
- Spray the stone with water to keep the dust down and the drill bit cool.

- submersible pump with water regulator set on high that moves 80 gallons (304l) per hour for the small and medium spheres; or a pump that moves 120 gallons (456l) per hour for the large sphere; or an 80-gallon pump for a large sphere with narrow tubing added inside the pump spout to compress the water, increasing the upward water pressure
- 1" (2.5cm) of flexible plastic tubing to fit your pump
- container in proportion to the size of your base and sphere
- rolling ball and predrilled base (small, medium or large)
- complementary-colored rocks, small and medium size and decorative accents

Rolling spheres, elegant additions to the fountain repertoire are currently imported from China and Brazil and are very difficult to replicate with home tools. Not only does the base socket need to match the sphere within $\frac{1}{32}$" (1mm), but the marble or granite sphere has to be perfectly round in order to spin. There is just one hole for the water to come out and spin the ball. With larger and heavier balls, the hole is drilled off center of the socket or depression to push water at an angle under the ball to start the spinning. Substituting a crystal ball or rose quartz ball generally doesn't work because the weight of

rolling sphere fountain

the sphere seems to play a part. Check the Resources section on pages 126-127 for purchasing information.

For this fountain I've chosen reddish brown stones, red and gold tinged slate chips, an ochre bowl and yellow calcite accents. The marble sphere is 1½" (3.8cm) in diameter on a 4" (10.2cm) tall rainbow rock base.

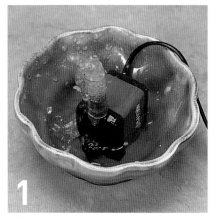

1 Set the Pump
Put the pump in the bowl, set the water flow regulator on high, and put 1" (2.5cm) of flexible tubing over the spout. Add water and turn it on. After assuring yourself the pump is working, unplug it.

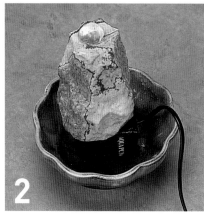

2 Add Drilled Stone Base
Set the drilled stone base on top of the pump and tubing.

3 Add Sphere
Set the sphere on top of the stone base. It should begin spinning.

accessorizing your sphere and base

Marble balls or spheres come in all kinds of earth tones: brown; reddish brown; white streaked with pink, blue, or gray; or all white. The bases are of rainbow rock (cream color with dark reddish brown streaks or patterns), marble (white, white with gray), quartz, blue sodalite and other minerals.

What color combination are you looking for? Review a color wheel to see what colors are complementary to the main color you want. Or visit a paint store and look at color charts with main color and trim suggestions. Use these guides as you select the fountain container, stones to fill your fountain and the accent pieces for this and other fountain projects.

Consider the proportions. Do you want a tall base in a small bowl? A shorter and wider base in a larger bowl? In an oval bowl, a base and sphere that takes up one end will offer more room for decorating the center and other end of the bowl. Would you want a clear pool in the center and another rise of rocks at the other end?

Consider the location of the fountain. An entry way, for instance could probably handle a large bowl, base and sphere, while a desktop might do better with a small bowl, tall base and small sphere. The largest spheres are about 3" (7.6cm) in diameter with a 4" (10.2cm) tall base (5" or 12.7cm wide). (Rose quartz or sodalite will cost more than rainbow rock.) The medium size sphere is about 2¼" (5.7cm) in diameter with a base 3" (7.6cm) tall and 3" wide. The smallest sphere, which I've used here, is 1½" (3.8cm) in diameter on a base 4" (10.2 cm) tall and 2¼" (5.7cm) wide.

Also consider the evaporation rate. A rolling sphere exposes a lot of water to the air; hence the evaporation is high and the bowl may need to be refilled every two days. The level of maintenance may help you decide on the size of bowl.

4 Add Rocks

Mound larger rocks near the pump, then add smaller stones around the edges. Put polished stones on top, arranging them attractively. Plug the pump in and watch the water spin the ball. You may have to give it a spin with your hand.

The Rolling Sphere fountain provides kinetic, visual and aural pleasure. As a desktop fountain, it stimulates ideas at work.

- submersible pump with water regulator set on high
- 6" (15.2cm) of flexible plastic tubing to fit your pump spout
- large 3" (7.6cm) deep basin or watersealed terra-cotta saucer
- underwater light with red cover
- fogger or mister
- large lava chunk with hole
- medium lava chunk with hole
- smaller lava pieces
- Sedona red stones and other decorative stones
- bromeliad in plastic pot inside a terra-cotta pot
- terra-cotta sealant
- epoxy putty
- latex gloves

Molten lava erupts from a volcano, slowly hardening into irregular shapes. Take advantage of the holes in lava rocks

lava rock fountain

to make your own lava fountain with water flowing down the surface and steam emerging from the volcano's base. Because you have to waterseal the bowl, allow for a drying time of two to eight hours before you start assembling your fountain.

1 Prepare the Bowl

Waterseal the terra-cotta saucer with terra-cotta sealant, concrete and masonry sealant or sprayed polyurethane (several coats, following the directions on the can). Let it dry thoroughly. Next put the pump in the bowl. Add 5" to 6" (12.7 to 15.2cm) of flexible tubing to elevate the water to the top of the volcano. Set the underwater light with red cover near the pump. Put the fogger beside the light.

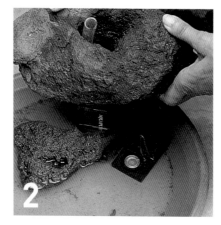

2 Put Lava Rock on Pump

Begin building the fountain centerpiece by sliding the lava chunk onto the back of the pump. Prop up the overhang with another piece of lava.

3 Add Small Stones

Cover the bottom of the bowl with handfuls of small stones, leaving a space for the plant.

4 Add Smaller Lava Rock

Add the second, smaller lava with hole on top of the first. If needed, slip small stones in between the two rocks to balance the design. Leave a space to the side of the lava rock for the plant.

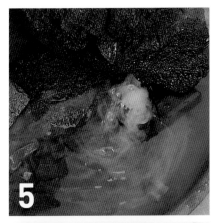

5 Add Water, Turn on Fountain
Add water and plug in the pump, underwater light with a red cover and fogger.

6 Put Rocks Behind Fogger
The fog will escape out the back, so put rocks in the open spaces behind the fogger to keep the fog in the front.

7 Put Rocks Around Fogger
The red light on the fogger indicates that it is working. Keep the fogger 1" to 4" (2.5 to 10.2cm) below the surface of the water according to the manufacturer's instructions. Put more rocks around the fogger to conceal the red light. Position the underwater light with red cover so it glows from within the lava rock.

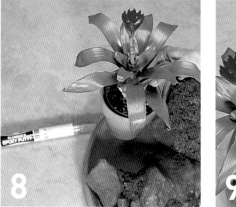  

8 Add Plant

A red bromeliad continues the tropical theme of smoking volcano and submerged red embers. Select a clay pot that complements the saucer color, and plug the clay pot's drainage hole with epoxy putty (wear latex gloves). Keep the bromeliad in its original plastic pot and put it into the clay pot. The plant won't take in too much water because it is sheltered by the extra pot. Set the plant next to the lava rock waterfall.

9 Adjust Water Flow

Adjust the flow of the water by lifting up the tubing as it comes out the top lava rock.

10 Add Small Stones

Wedge a small rock under the tip of the tubing to hold it upright and fill in other gaps at the top with small stones. Adjust the light, fogger and rocks until you are pleased with the sight and sound of your Lava Rock fountain.

This fountain would be an interesting addition to your family room where one and all can enjoy the special effects.

history of fountains

Fountains have a long and rich history because of their association with water, the essence of life. Water's many qualities have fascinated poets and philosophers. Water moves in waves, swirls, ripples, cascades and torrents, making it an elemental force of nature that can destroy as well as fertilize. Water can be a gas or solid; in its liquid state, it conducts electricity. When falling water droplets are sheared, water releases negative ions, which are said to produce better mood, concentration and sleep. Water is reflective like a mirror and also transparent.

Because of its transparency and depth, water is associated with the transition between air and earth. One creation myth from India, for instance, starts "In the beginning there was nothing but water, water, water…. As the sky is now, so then was water."

Water represents intuitive wisdom, the life force and fertility of spiritual life. In Psalm 36 we read, "for with thee is the fountain of life," and in Revelations 21:6, "the fountain of the river of life." Water has come to be associated with baptism, ritual cleansing and purification.

In the West, particularly in Renaissance Italy, water is linked to an outpouring of reserves. River god fountain statues, for example, often hold overflowing cornucopias. In the exuberant Renaissance, water's abundant possibilities were expressed in jets and cascades, such as those at the Villa d'Este. Water is also associated with the moon and the feminine and with shrines and grottoes (caves with water, such as the Grotto of Lourdes).

materials

- submersible pump with water regulator set on low
- oversized latte cup, soup mug or cereal bowl
- straw basket
- sheets of plastic and aluminum foil
- flat stone, such as sandstone
- medium plastic lid from cottage cheese or similar container
- polished rocks or beach stones
- Spanish moss or other filler
- decorative accents, such as eucalyptus sprig, crystals or driftwood
- animal accents, such as a bird or frog
- craft knife

People look twice when they see water bubbling in a straw basket. You can use a picnic basket with its hinged lid held

basket fountain

upright in back, a round basket with two handles hanging from the sides or a basket with an arching handle, such as the one pictured here. The trick is to create your fountain in a bowl or cup!

1 Put Pump in Mug

Start by putting the pump in your mug. Add water to make sure the mug holds enough water to cover the intake valve.

2 Line Basket

While assembling the fountain, water is likely to splash out of the cup into the basket, so it is wise to line the basket with plastic.

3 Position the Cup

Aluminum foil on the bottom and sides of the basket provides an additional layer of protection. Your mug may not be level with the sides of the basket when you put it in, so you may need to elevate it with a flat rock or crumpled aluminum foil.

4 Cut the Lid

A plastic lid placed over the pump spout is a technique that keeps the water in the cup from evaporating as quickly. The fountain will need refilling less often if there is water recirculating below the lid. Use a knife to cut an X in the lid off center so it will fit over the spout.

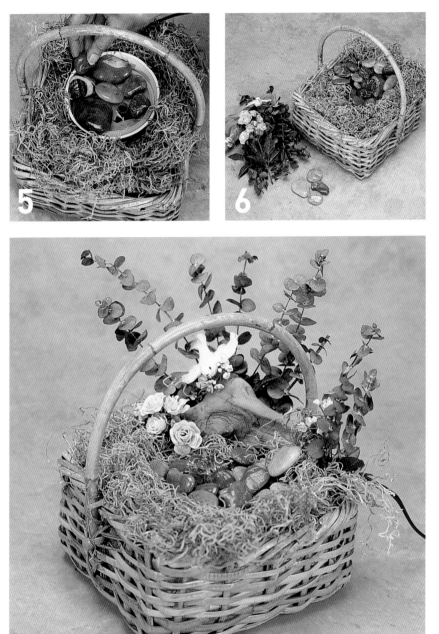

A white dove adds character to this bubbling spring in a secluded wood. This fountain would look terrific on a counter or hearth. Just looking at the contemplative setting of your hand-crafted fountain will have a calming effect.

5 Add Stones and Moss

Place polished stones or beach stones on the lid making sure the lid stays level. Add moss to the open areas of the basket.

6 Arrange the Moss

Work with your arrangement, packing or lifting the moss so the fountain stones stand out. Gather your decorative accents and decide how best to arrange them. Dark green eucalyptus stems add a vertical line, while tiny baby's breath adds contrast.

7 Add Wood, Moss and Stones

A weather-beaten piece of wood anchors the composition. Disguise the cord with moss or wood. Camouflage the rim of the mug with polished stones or small rocks, taking care that the water doesn't run over them into the moss. Angle stones against the spout so the water doesn't spray out.

- small submersible pump with water regulator set on high
- 2" (5.1cm) of flexible plastic tubing to fit your pump spout
- bowl at least 3" (7.6cm) deep
- Y-attachment to fit tubing
- 2 conch-type shells (spiral, univalve) about 4" (10.2cm) long
- 3 flat, drilled stones, sizes small, medium, and large
- stones
- shell, stone or driftwood
- small flat stones
- other small shells
- air plant or other accents
- concrete and masonry sealant
- epoxy putty (optional)
- paints and conditioner
- scissors
- latex gloves (optional)

Create an atmosphere of tropical calm right in your home or office with water flowing from seashells. Shells, emblems of good luck and prosperous journeys, are easy to

two shells fountain

work with and are a natural for a beach scene fountain. Although this project doesn't involve drilling, shells are easy to drill with a cone-shaped ceramic rotary tool bit. Wear nose and eye protection if you drill a shell because the dust is very unpleasant.

1 Paint the Bowl

If you don't like the color of your bowl, you can easily change it with a variety of paints. I used Perm Enamel conditioner and De-coArt paints, mixing colors to get a brownish tan. Waterseal the terra-cotta bowl afterward to preserve the paint, using concrete and masonry sealant, Perm Enamel Clear Gloss Glaze or clear polyurethane spray.

2 Fill Hole in Bowl, Add Pump

If your bowl has a drainage hole, fill it with a thin layer of epoxy putty. While wearing latex gloves, break off a small piece from the putty tube, mush it together to combine the epoxy and putty, flatten it with your fingers, place over the hole and press down the edges. It will dry in about an hour.

If your plastic tubing is curved, refer to page 10 for instructions on straightening it. With sharp scissors, cut about 2" (5.1cm) of flexible plastic tubing to fit over the pump spout and put the pump in the center of the bowl. Add water and turn on the pump to be sure it works.

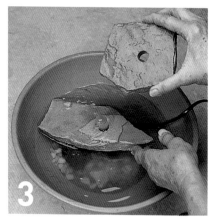

3 Drill Stones

Unplug the pump and begin stacking the drilled stones. (If you need instructions in drilling stone, refer to Drilling on page 21.) Drilling sandstone takes considerably longer than slate if the sandstone has tiny crystals in it. The medium-size piece goes on first, then the small one over it. The small stone should be just above the water level in the bowl.

4 Stack Stones on Pump

The large drilled stone goes on top. If water escapes from the Y-attachment, it will flow over the large platform rock and curve under to land on the recessed rocks, creating an interesting water flow pattern.

5 Add Rocks Underneath

To stabilize the three drilled pieces, slip rocks under the lowest drilled rock. Use a few rocks to prop up an uneven tilt so the platform is level.

6 Hide the Cord

Pebbles scattered about add a naturalistic touch to a water-washed beach. Hide the cord as it exits the bowl by placing a shell, stone or driftwood piece over it.

7 Add the Y

Put the long end of the Y-attachment into the pump spout and press it down firmly.

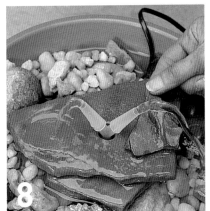

8 Turn On Pump

Add water and plug in the pump to see what the lift and distance of the water jets are as the water comes out in two streams. Probably one is higher than the other, and that side is the one to build up so water will catch in the shell and not shoot over it. Build up that side by adding a few flat stone chips for the shell to rest on.

9 Position the Shells

Balance the two shells on either side of the Y, facing opposite directions. The tips of the Y-attachment just reach over the edges of the shells. Secure the shells by pushing pebbles around them where they sit on the platform. Later you may want to glue the arrangement in place. Shift the shells around so water fills the shells and flows out the shell lips into the bowl below.

10 Add Foliage

Add air plants or other decorative accents.

11 Cover the Y

Finish by covering the Y. Lean two scallop shells or flat rock chips on either side of the Y to hide the water source.

Your friends will wonder where the water is coming from. This fountain would look good in a bedroom or on your office desk.

the symbolism of water

Water is associated with the second chakra, representing creativity and passion, and with three signs in astrology—Pisces, Cancer and Scorpio. In ancient Greece, healing temples were built near natural springs, while in ancient Egypt and the Near East, spring water was channeled under pressure for irrigation. Later the channels became pools with pavilions, prized for their decorative and cooling effects. Over the centuries garden fountains became areas for sanctuary and retreat, pleasant settings for music, poetry and art.

In the Far East, designers used falling water and streams to re-create nature in miniature, asymmetrical and serene. The sixth century B.C. philosopher Lao-tzu observed, "Nothing in the world is as soft and yielding as water. Yet for dissolving the hard and inflexible, nothing can surpass it." Feng Shui, the ancient Chinese art of placement, means "wind-water." The art describes how to harmonize the elements to create abundance, prosperity and positive energy in the environment.

The English language also associates moving water with money: cash flow, slush fund, washed up, float a loan, liquid assets, money spigot, frozen assets, bank (as in river), pool your money, flush with money, laundered money, money down the drain. These are some American phrases linking money and water. What do you think of when the image of water comes to mind?

- submersible pump with spout that fits ⅝" o.d. tubing, water regulator set on high
- about 12" (30.5cm) (long enough to reach through the top pot) of ⅝" (16mm) o.d. **rigid** plastic tubing
- ¾" (19mm) of ⅝" (16mm) o.d. **flexible** plastic tubing
- ¾" (19mm) ½" (13mm) o.d. **flexible** plastic tubing (optional)
- ¾" (19mm) of ¾" (19mm) o.d. **flexible** plastic tubing
- 2 or 3 terra-cotta garden pots in diminishing sizes with saucers
- PVC collar
- white plastic fluorescent light grid
- drilled slate
- polished stones
- slate pieces
- white or earth-toned pebbles or small shells
- terra-cotta sealant
- epoxy putty or E6000 glue
- DecoArt acrylic paints in colors of your choice and DecoArt Conditioner (primer)
- marking pen
- dust mask
- latex gloves
- round file or rotary tool with ceramic drilling bit
- hacksaw
- craft scissors (optional)

Clay pots of matching style and diminishing size are often stocked at garden centers, pottery stores and home decorating shops. Look for pots that will fit inside each other and have room for water to flow over the edge without overshooting the bowl below. I found two pots at a garden center that had streaks of shiny gray and copper in the terra-cotta that added a metallic glint, but my base container was a lighter color and didn't match. I decided to paint the base to match the smaller pots. I learned that it is difficult to match metallics; an easier solution would have

tiered clay pot fountain

been to paint all the pots the same color. Painting your containers enables you to customize your fountain to blend with your decor.

1 Seal Bottom Pot

If you don't plan to paint the pots, waterseal them with terra-cotta sealant, concrete sealant, or polyurethane liquid or spray (pictured). Use four or five coats of spray sealant on the bottom container.

2 Assemble Paints

If you plan to paint your pots, paint them before watersealing them. DecoArt paints are great for painting clay and terra-cotta because they wash up with water, come in a variety of solid and metallic colors, dry quickly and blend easily. Using a conditioner first helps the paint adhere to the surface.

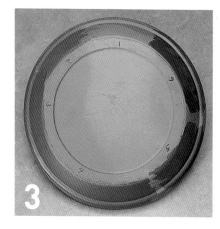

3 Test Your Paint on Bottom of Saucer

The formulas arrayed around the saucer show my experiments with matching tints. The final formula is two parts Venetian Gold, two parts Emperor Gold, one part Burnt Umber and one part Chocolate. When you've blended the formula that best matches or complements the color of your tiered pots, apply conditioner first, then paint the outside of the containers and saucer. When the paint dries, waterseal the pots, especially the bottom container.

4 Plug Hole

Use epoxy putty or E6000 to fill the drainage hole in the large pot. As always, wear latex gloves to work with the adhesive.

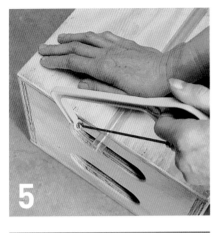

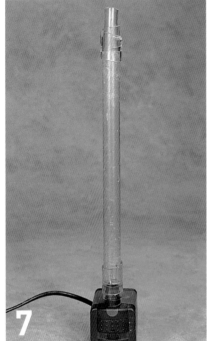

5 Cut Tubing

Measure the length of rigid ⅝" (16mm) tubing you'll need by loosely stacking the pots on top of the pump. Hold the tubing upright by the base of the first tier and mark with a pen where to cut off the excess tubing. Use a small sharp saw or hacksaw for plastics and with short strokes, cut the rigid tubing.

6 Connect or Glue Tubing

The ¾" (19mm) o.d. tubing is a connector piece between the ⅝" (16mm) flexible tubing and the ⅝" rigid tubing. The rigid tubing is a little loose for the pump spout, so the connector piece joins the two kinds of ⅝" tubing. Set the pump water regulator on high.

You can use E6000 to glue the rigid tubing directly to the pump spout, but then you can't use the pump spout in another fountain. Also you'll need to wait twenty-four hours for the E6000 to dry completely and you may be eager to proceed.

7 Add Flexible Tubing (optional)

Insert the ½" (13mm) flexible tubing into the top of the rigid tubing to give a little extra plume of water above the second tier. The smaller-diameter tubing compresses the water, raising its height.

8 Position Collar Around Pump

The collar provides a secure base for the slate and pots to rest on. Drop a PVC collar around the pump with the cord coming out of one of the bottom notches. Or glue bottle caps to the bottom of the PVC collar to elevate it so the cord can get out and the water can get into the pump.

9 Put Pump Assembly in Bowl

Put your pump assembly with the water flow on high into the bottom container. Fill with water and plug in the pump to be sure it works. Thread a piece of drilled slate (see Drilling on page 21) over the tubing so it rests on the PVC collar.

10 Direct the Water Flow

Next, the drainage holes of your tiered pots will probably need to be enlarged to fit snugly over the rigid tubing. A round file or rotary tool with ceramic bit will grind away excess clay and make the hole bigger. Try fitting the pot over the rigid tubing as you grind or drill so you don't cut away too much clay. Wear a dust mask; dip the pot in water as you drill to keep the bit cool.

11 Make Grid Tray

You can fill the first-tier bowl with stones or you can make a tray so your fountain will be lighter and you won't need so many stones. Using a tip from Terry Crawford, fountain maker from Oregon, I cut a tray from a white plastic fluorescent light grid. The ½" (13mm) squares allow stones to be stacked on the cover while water flows through the squares to pool in the first-tier bowl and then rises to overflow the edges. This overflow gives the pouring effect you want. Invert the first-tier pot on the grid and outline it with a black pen.

12 Fit Grid in Bowl

Using medium heavy-duty craft scissors cut abut 1½" to 2" (3.8 to 5.1cm) inside the black line. It is pretty tough to cut, so take it slowly. Then trim out a few squares in the center for the rigid tubing to go through. Fit the plastic circle inside the first-tier bowl. It should be about ¾" (19mm) inside the rim so it will hold the polished stones.

13 Fit Bowl on Tubing

Then slide the first-tier bowl over the rigid tubing until it rests on the slate. If the drainage hole is too small to fit over the tubing, use a rotary tool with a cone-shaped ceramic bit to enlarge the hole.

14 Add Tray

Slide the white plastic grid over the tubing to rest inside the first-tier bowl.

15 Add Stones

Mound the polished stones on the tray and level them so the next-tier pot will have a stable base.

16 Add Next Tier

Slide the second-tier pot over the tubing and wiggle it around on the polished rocks so it is level. Fill the second pot with polished stones or pebbles. The narrow ½" (13mm) tubing should stick up just above the stones.

17 Add Slate Pieces

Begin filling the container with slate pieces. Slide them in so they touch the PVC collar in the center of the bowl and form irregular ledges below the drilled slate. You can adjust the angle of the first-tier bowl by adding pebbles under it to prop it up or lean it in toward the center of the bowl.

18 Add Decorative Stones

As a finishing touch, add white or earth-toned pebbles or small shells to the second-tier pot and along the slate ledges.

19 Adjust the Water Flow

Add water if needed, plug in the pump and notice where and how the water flows. Tilt the pots if you want water to flow in a certain direction, or level the pots if you want water to flow uniformly over the edges.

Here the pots are set toward the back of the bowl and are tilted forward so the water streams mostly in one direction and the slate ledges are in the foreground.

This fountain would look great in a sunroom or garden. It is large enough to be the focal point of a foyer as well.

8. Tape the cord to a table leg as it descends to the outlet.

9. Tape the cord to the carpet or floor and throw a rug over the cord when it is on the floor and on its way to the electrical outlet.

10. Use a pump that has a thin cord (two-prong plug) rather than the thicker outdoor three-prong plug. The Hagen Aqua Pump and other aquarium pumps have thin cords.

ten ways to hide the cord

1. Build the fountain up in back so the cord exits out of view over the bowl's edge, hidden by a vertical stone, for instance.

2. Put spider plant cuttings, silk flowers or ivy in the fountain bowl so they drape over the edge where the cord exits the bowl's edge, disguising the cord.

3. Use a telephone wire clip with adhesive back (from office supply stores) to fasten the cord to the outside of the bowl.

4. If using a black bowl, tape the cord to the bowl with black electrical tape.

5. Circle the cord around the base of the bowl so it will lie flat on its way to the electrical outlet.

6. Place a plant or flowers on the table by the bowl where the cord comes down.

7. Run the cord under a doily or scarf after it leaves the bowl and is on the table (that is, covering the cord).

uses for a fountain
- create a peaceful, natural indoor environment
- make a centerpiece for a home altar
- craft a unique gift suitable for any occasion
- set the tone for meditation
- humidify dry air
- relax you into sleep

materials

- submersible pump with water regulator set on low
- flexible plastic tubing to fit your pump spout, length suitable for depth of gourd
- 5" (12.7cm) coil of ⅜" (10mm) o.d. copper refrigerator tubing
- dried gourd with round base at least 8" (20.3cm) in diameter and 6" (15.2cm) tall after cutting
- 18" (45.7cm) of 16-gauge (3mm) copper wire
- small slate pieces about 1" to 2" (2.5 to 5.1cm) long
- slate piece about 3" (7.6cm) long
- feathers, beads, small shells, pine needles (optional)
- colorful stones (aqua cove, turquoise, rose quartz) or luster gems (optional)
- polyurethane clear sealant
- polyurethane clear finish, carnauba wax, or varnish
- acrylic paints, leather dyes, permanent markers, oil pastels or watercolors
- cotton cloth (optional)
- old spoon or grapefruit spoon
- dust mask
- latex or rubber gloves
- sandpaper, wood rasp or fine steel wool (optional)
- copper mesh scrubber
- keyhole saw or craft knife
- awl or thin, sharp knife
- wire cutters or needle nose pliers (optional)

Gourds have been used for hundreds of years to carry and store water, so why not make a fountain out of one? Look for many decorative techniques using woodburning, paint-

gourd fountain

ing, weaving, and mosaic in *The Complete Book of Gourd Craft* by Ginger Summit, Jim Widess and Deborah Morgenthal. Thanks to Carol E. Lang of Carlsbad, California, for her Gourd Art Class and to Sammie Crawford, the Fairy Gourdmother™, gourd artist and author of *Gourd Fun for Everyone* by North Light Books, for the gourds used in this project.

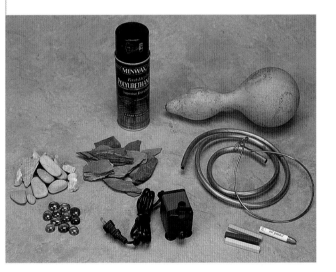

1 Select a Gourd

Gourds come in many sizes and shapes. You will need a dried gourd. During the drying process, the gourd will turn black and moldy looking, but don't worry, that's what you want. The gourd is properly dried if it is lightweight and the seeds rattle inside.

2 Clean the Gourd

You will need to clean the mold off the gourd. Gourd dust is irritating to the lungs, so wear a mask for scrubbing and cutting the gourd. Scrub it with a mesh scrubber and water or water and a little bleach. You may have to soak the gourd in water for an hour and then scrape it to remove every last bit of mold.

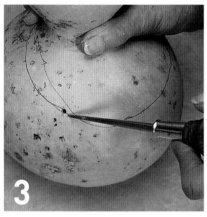

3 Start the Cut

Look your gourd over to decide how you will cut it to make a bowl: higher in back, lower in front; cut in scallops or waves, cut straight across or cut out an oval. Draw with pencil where you will cut. Gently twisting the awl, ease the tip through the gourd skin at a place on the line. Or use a thin, sharp craft knife with nonretractable handle to begin the cut.

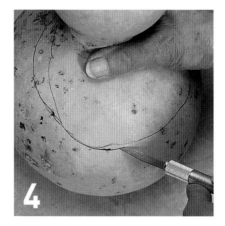

4 Cut the Gourd

Once you have the gourd pierced, use a key-hole saw or craft knife fitted with a saw blade to cut on the line. Use quick, short strokes to cut the gourd. If the blade sticks, back it off a little and resume sawing.

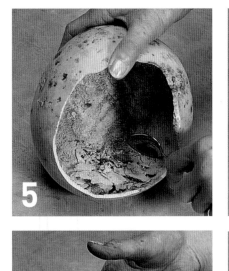

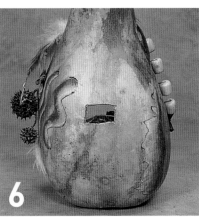

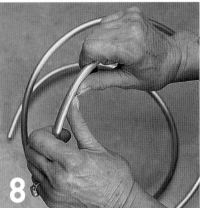

5 Scrape the Inside

Clean the inside with an old spoon or grapefruit spoon with jagged edge. Get off as much loose fiber as you can, but don't scrape so hard you break the gourd shell. Smooth the cut edges with sandpaper, a wood rasp, or fine steel wool. Now waterseal the inside of the gourd with polyurethane spray (three to four coats) or liquid (one to two coats).

6 Cut Hole in Back

If you have chosen a gourd with a tall back, drill then cut a hole in the back for the cord and plug to leave the container. Later you can pile up rocks in the gourd container in front of the hole to hide it, or cover the opening with an air plant.

7 Color the Gourd

You can use a variety of materials to color the gourd, such as acrylic paints, leather dyes, permanent markers or watercolors. This project shows blue, light green and dark green wax pastel crayons from an art store. Cover the whole container with one color, blending with your finger or cotton cloth for an even hue. Then cover with a second color, moving the pastel crayon back and forth over the gourd. Again blend the colors. Repeat with the third color until you have a rich, shiny surface. Seal the surface with polyurethane clear finish, carnauba wax, varnish or other sealant and let it dry.

8 Make the Stand

The idea for a stand comes from **The Complete Book of Gourd Craft,** which uses a coil of copper refrigerator tubing. Working with the coil, increase the curve by bending the copper, with thumbs together and pulling down slightly. Then pull the coil up slightly to create a spiral.

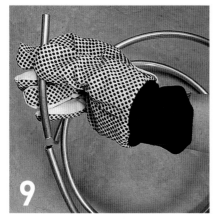

9 Cut Off Excess Tubing

If the copper spiral is too long, cut off the excess using the copper tube cutting technique on page 11.

10 Adjust Stand

Place the gourd on the stand and adjust the copper spiral until the gourd fits.

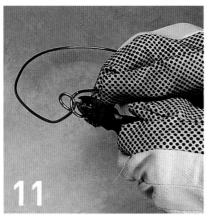

11 Make Necklace

Wrap the 16-gauge (3mm) copper wire around the gourd for a necklace, and cut with wire cutters, leaving about 5" (12.7cm) extra to make a curl to connect the ends. Using the tip of the wire cutters or needle nose pliers, curl back each end and then slip the curls together, making a clasp.

12 Adjust Necklace

Drape the necklace over the gourd and adjust it to fit. You can also add beads or feathers to the curls of the necklace for more embellishment. Remove the necklace while you assemble the fountain.

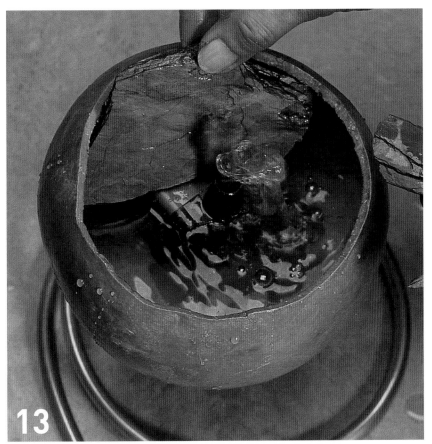

13 Begin Assembling Fountain

If your gourd is small, set the pump's water regulator to low and set the pump in the gourd. Add water. Add slate pieces to the bottom and behind the pump to hide the cord as it goes over the edge of the gourd.

14 Add Rocks

Add decorative rocks over the slate pieces. If your gourd is tall, add a length of flexible tubing to your pump spout to elevate the water.

15 Add Semi-Precious Stones

The blue-green of the gourd will be complemented by adding semiprecious stones, such as turquoise and landscape variety aqua cove pebbles.

16 Add Luster Gems

Iridescent blue-green luster gems add sparkle and highlights. Tuck them into corners where they won't slip to the bottom of the bowl.

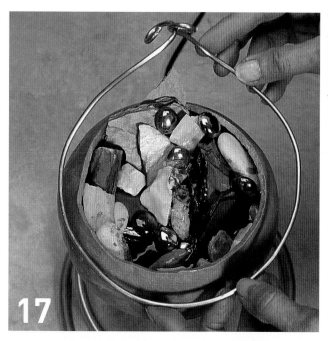

17 Add Necklace to the Gourd

Adjust the copper necklace as a finishing touch. If the copper tarnishes, clean it with salt and lemon juice; or seal the copper with a spray polyurethane or lacquer to keep it shining brightly.

This fountain is small enough to become a desktop fountain in your office at work or at home. The soothing sounds of the water will mask computer noises and contribute to a pleasant, creative environment. The low setting on the pump means the water sound is a gentle murmur.

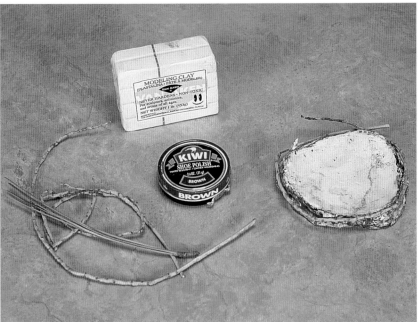

Another stand to balance the gourd and keep it upright can be made from plasticene modeling clay. Flatten a chunk of clay, put the gourd on the clay and press the clay up around the base of the gourd. Color the clay wall with shoe polish, permanent marker or acrylic paint. Press pine needles (softened by soaking in water for five minutes), shells, buttons or other accents into the clay.

This variation of the Gourd fountain shows that a tall gourd with different embellishments creates a unique look. The natural color patches of the gourd were enhanced by woodburned outlines, and holes were drilled around the opening to attach feathers and other decorations. The base is made from plasticene clay, as described above.

- submersible pump with spout that fits ⅝" (16mm) o.d. flexible plastic tubing, with water regulator set on low
- short piece of ⅝" (16mm) o.d. flexible plastic tubing
- short piece of ½" (12mm) o.d. flexible plastic tubing
- 12" (30.4cm) of rigid copper pipe ⅝" (16mm) o.d.
- copper elbow that fits the pipe
- copper end cap that fits the pipe
- fountain bowl
- 18" (45.7cm) of 16-gauge (3mm) copper wire
- 3" (7.6cm) wide and 4" (10.2cm) long piece of slate
- one heavy stone
- rocks
- ivy sprigs
- spray lacquer (optional)
- E6000 glue (optional)
- electrical tape or vise
- latex gloves
- metal pipe cutter or rotary tool with metal pipe cutting wheels (disks)
- variable-speed electric drill with ⅛" (3mm) and 1/16" (2mm) drill bits
- hammer
- awl
- wire cutters
- needle nose pliers

Hanging slate fountains have a special charm. There is movement not only in the water but also in the object on which it flows. The slate sways gently in the wind and water, a sure sign good chi has been called. Some hanging slate styles are quite sophisticated and require metal-working skills. This project is well within reach of beginning fountain builders.

Instead of slate, you might find a glazed ceramic tile to

hanging slate fountain

use for the centerpiece. Ceramic tile drilling instructions are on page 78.

Begin by setting up the bowl. Put flexible tubing on the spout, and set the pump in the bowl so the spout is near the bowl edge. This will give more room across the bowl for the horizontal bar than if you put the pump in the middle. If your pump has suction cup feet, press down to secure them. This fountain will need all the anchoring you can give it because the weight of the copper bar and the slate tend to tilt the pump in the direction of the weight.

Set the water flow regulator on low. Next determine how tall you want the vertical copper piece in proportion to the size and shape of your bowl. About 7" (17.8cm) is good for a bowl 14" (35.6cm) in diameter. The crosspiece is 4" long (10cm).

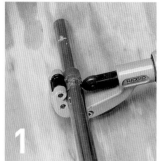

1 Cut Copper Pipe
Cut the copper pipe with a special metal pipe-cutting tool (pictured) or with a rotary tool fitted with two metal sawing disks (see page 11).

2 Stabilize the Short Pipe
Use a vise to hold the shorter pipe stable or tape it between the vertical piece and a length of ⅝" (16mm) tubing or another copper tube. This way the pipe won't rotate as you start hammering. Pencil a line down the length of the shorter pipe so the holes will line up. Mark places for six drip holes in the center 4" (10.2cm) pipe, referring to the photo in step 6 for placement.

3 Make Starter Holes
Twist the awl into the marked tape to make a starter scratch so the awl won't slip when you make the holes.

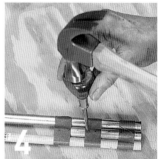

4 Make Holes in the Copper Crosspiece
Tap forcefully with the hammer until the awl penetrates the copper about ⅛" (3mm). Be careful not to hammer all the way through to the other side. Or use a ⅛" drill bit on your variable-speed electric drill and stop drilling once the bit has penetrated the copper.

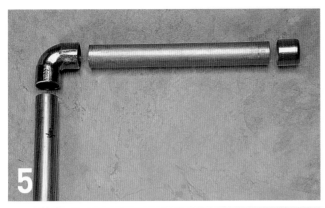

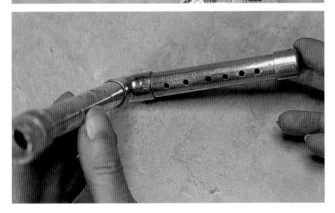

5 Lay Out Pieces

Lay out the ⅞" (22mm) tubing, vertical pipe, elbow, pipe with holes and end cap.

6 Glue Pieces Together

Cut a piece of ½" (12mm) flexible plastic tubing to join the copper pipe with the ⅝" (16mm) tubing that is on the pump spout. This connector tubing will enclose the vertical copper pipe and smaller tubing. The alternative is to glue the pump spout directly to the copper tubing, but then you can't use the pump spout for another fountain. Put on latex gloves and glue the pieces together, making sure the holes are on the under-side. Let the glue dry for four to twelve hours. If you like the shiny copper, you can spray it with lac-quer so it won't darken.

7 Place Assembly in Bowl
Put the assembly on the pump and weigh down the pump casing with a heavy stone. Wedge rocks around the pump.

8 Add Rocks
Continue adding stones to the pump area, bracing the copper pipe so it will remain upright.

9 Add Water, Plants and More Rocks
Add water and plug in the pump. Decide which rocks you want to place below the hanging slate. This example uses sunburst cobblestones, a rich orange when wet. Add ivy sprigs for green color.

Using the slate-shaping technique of tapping with a hammer (see page 20), shape the outline of your 3" x 4" (7.6 to 10.2cm) slate piece that will hang from the bar. There are many shaping results possible, including a V-shaped piece where the water comes together at that point and runs off in one stream and a level bottom where the water drips off all across the lower edge.

About ½" (13mm) from the top of the slate piece, drill two small holes with a 7⁄8" (2mm) drill bit in a variable-speed drill. If you drill closer to the edge, the slate may crack.

Cut about 5" (12.7cm) from the copper wire and bend into a ring. Slip the ring into one hole in the slate. With needle nose pliers, twist the ends together, making sure the ring and slate can fit over the horizontal bar. Make a second ring for the other hole and trim excess wire with wire cutters.

If the holes in the horizontal bar are uneven and water shoots in different directions instead of straight down, try hanging two thin pieces of slate threaded on three rings. This will give extra width to the slate so water is sure to touch the slate surface and it looks just as attractive as the single piece of slate.

10 Put Slate on Copper Tube

Slide both rings over the horizontal copper bar, and watch the water run down the slate! If the copper tarnishes, clean it occasionally with salt and lemon juice.

Putting this fountain in your bedroom may help lull you to sleep. If the sound becomes disturbing after awhile, according to Feng Shui, the fountain has done its job shifting the room's energy and may be moved to another room.

64

materials

- submersible pump with spout that fits ⅝" (16mm) tubing, with water regulator set on medium
- 8" to 10" (20.3 to 25.4cm) ½" (13mm) o.d. rigid plastic tubing
- flexible plastic tubing: 1" (2.5cm) of ⅝" (16mm) o.d., 1" (2.5cm) of ¾" (19mm) o.d.
- teapot or other container
- brass or plastic faucet from hardware store, with a ¾" (19mm) opening so tubing fits just inside the faucet
- ½" (13mm) wood or Plexiglas dowel
- heavy round stones
- E6000 glue or other underwater adhesive
- latex gloves
- small saw with sharp blade or craft knife
- awl or variable-speed electric drill with 1⁄16" (2mm) drill bit
- clamp or other brace

This unusual fountain with a faucet floating in midair sends a stream of water to the teapot below. You could also use a watering can, pail or even a metal tub with saucers and

magic fountain

plates being washed. One consideration is keeping the stiff plastic tubing vertical. Another is making a flange or projecting rim on the round tubing to hold it in place and attach it to the faucet. The result? Water comes up inside the tube and flows down the outside of the tube, surprising one and all the first time they see it.

1 Insert Pump

Start by putting your pump in the teapot or other container. Determine where you want the faucet to be in the air and slide the pump spout so it will be under the faucet. If your pump has suction cups, press down on the pump to anchor it.

2 Determine Tubing Length

The tube should be about 8" to 10" (20.3 to 25.4cm) above the rim of the container to show off the floating faucet. If you are using a deep pail, set the water pressure on high to pump the water up to the faucet. (You may find you need a stronger pump.) Test the fit of the stiff tubing into the faucet.

3 Cut Tubing

Saw off the length of ½" (13mm) o.d. rigid tubing you want to use (see page 11). Scissors will compress and crack the rigid tubing, but they are great for cutting the flexible tubing for the connecting pieces, 1" (2.5cm) of each of the ⅝" (16mm) and ¾" (19mm) o.d. tubing.

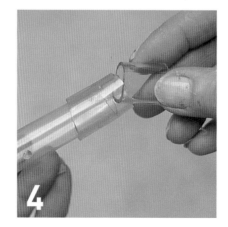

4 Connect Tubing

Fit the ¾" (19mm) tubing over one end of the rigid tubing to act as a connector between the rigid tubing and the flexible tubing that goes over the pump spout. Then fit the smaller ⅝" (16mm) tubing inside of the ¾" tubing.

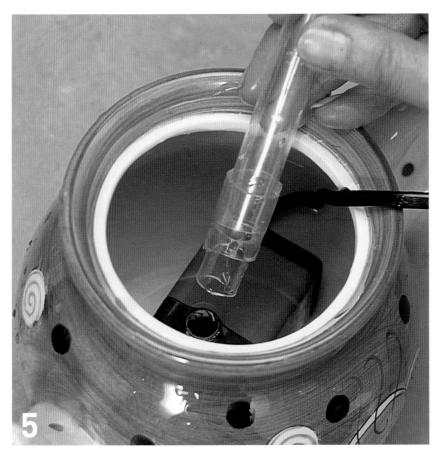

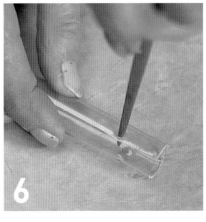

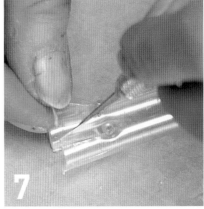

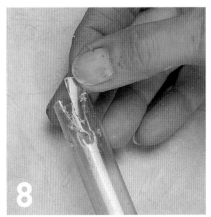

5 Fit Tubing on Pump

You can glue the rigid tubing directly onto the pump spout with E6000. However, if you do that you can't use the pump spout for another project. See how well the tubing assembly fits on the pump spout. Wiggle and twist it until you can make the tubing perfectly vertical.

6 Make Holes in Tubing

Measure about ¾" (19mm) down from the top of the rigid tubing. With an awl, gently press and twist six or eight small holes in the tubing, being careful not to split the plastic. To be safe, thread the rigid tubing on a dowel to support it as you make the holes. Or use a ¹⁄₁₆" (2mm) drill bit to drill the holes, clamping the tubing so it doesn't roll.

7 Make a Flange

Using a craft knife or saw, cut lines from the edge of the tubing down to the holes. Support the inside of the tubing with a dowel as you cut so the plastic doesn't collapse.

8 Flare the Tubing

Bend back the segments to widen the end of the tubing, making the flange.

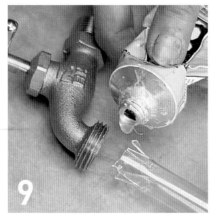

9 Glue Faucet to Tubing
Fit the tubing inside the faucet to make sure the segments are not spread out too far. Put on latex gloves and then squeeze E6000 into the faucet rim and around the edges of the tubing. Let the glue set for about ten minutes and then fit the two pieces together.

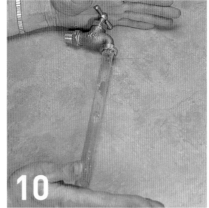

10 Let Dry
The tubing tends to pop out, so brace or clamp the tubing and faucet so they stay tightly together until dry (about twelve hours).

11 Assemble the Fountain
When the faucet and tubing are well glued, put the tubing on the pump spout. Add rocks around and on top of the pump to further stabilize it, and plug it in.

other tips and techniques:

- Make eight holes with the awl about ½" (13mm) from the end of the tubing. When the tubing is glued inside the faucet, water will shoot out the holes, hit the inside of the faucet and drop down the outside of the tubing. Faucet nozzles vary, so experiment to see what works.

- Another way to attach the tube is to drill many small holes in the end and attach with plumber's putty a piece of window screening that is formed to fit over the end of the tube. Put the screening only a little ways down the tube to allow enough water to come out of the drilled holes to evenly cover the tube. Use the same putty to attach the screen to the inside of the faucet. Also use the putty to plug the back end of the faucet and paint the putty to match the faucet.

- Drill out the spigot with a ½" (13mm) drill bit to accommodate the tube. This makes it easier to get it to support the valve while allowing enough room for the spray holes. Epoxy putty was used to glue the tube to the spigot, and window screening was stuffed around the tube to get the right flow.

12 Observe Water Flow

Water will be pumped up the inside of the tubing and then it will flow down the outside of the tubing. The water flowing outside the tubing hides the fact that water is flowing up inside, creating the magical effect of a faucet suspended in midair.

13 Adjust Water Pressure

Water may shoot out too forcefully from the slits and holes even when the water regulator is on low. Reduce the water pressure by making a hole with the awl in the tubing near the pump spout. Angle the hole up toward the faucet so water will be released downward. If you put the hole in straight, water may shoot out across the container and over the edge.

The finished fountain has the cord wrapped once around the base of the teapot. In the kitchen or breakfast area, you could set teacups and saucers around the fountain teapot.

- submersible pump with water regulator set on medium or high
- short connecting piece of flexible tubing to fit inside the bamboo and over the pump spout
- bowl at least 3" (7.6cm) deep
- 1" (2.5cm) diameter bamboo stake, 24" (61cm) long
- raffia
- stones and pebbles
- live bamboo shoots (optional)
- live plant (optional)
- decorative stones, such as turquoise, crystals or aqua cove (optional)
- marine varnish, polyurethane or carnauba wax (optional)
- E6000 glue (optional)
- marking pen
- rubber band
- latex gloves (optional)
- sharp saw
- craft knife or other sharp instrument

Bamboo fountains make a natural, relaxing water scene. My thanks to Anne Geldert, fountain maker in Ramona, CA, for the three vertical pipes idea. Water bubbles up one

bamboo fountain

section of the bamboo, falls into the holes of two other sections and into the pool below. Straw raffia ties the bamboo pieces, and live bamboo cuttings add a touch of green. This project does not require drilling.

In the Far East bamboo is thought to bring good fortune. In Buddhism the joints, individual segments and straight growth have additional symbolism.

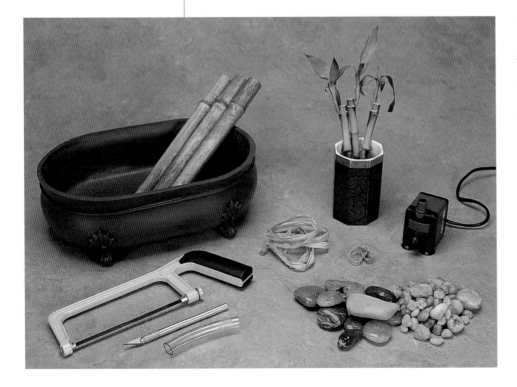

1 Clean Bamboo

Look for a bamboo pole or stake in garden centers or see Resources list for bamboo mail order. A piece about 1" (2.5cm) in diameter will fit best (or can be modified to fit) over the pump spout. Clean the bamboo if it has rain and dust streaks from sitting outside.

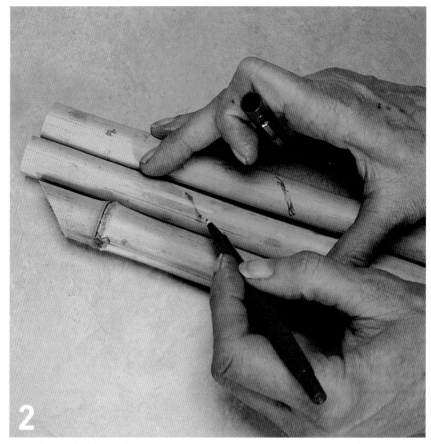

2 Cut Bamboo Into Three Pieces

With a sharp saw, cut the bamboo stake into three pieces, each with a growth ring: tall (about 8" or 20.3cm), medium (about 6" or 15.2cm), and short (about 4" or x10.2cm). Line up the three pieces. The tallest piece should have the growth ring near the top so it can be easily punctured for water to flow through. The middle piece should have the growth ring about halfway down so water can flow into it, fill it up and overflow. If the growth ring is too near the top where water flows into it, the water will quickly fill up the bamboo and splash out. The shortest piece should have the growth ring near the bottom so the ring will show as an attractive detail and also allow the water to pool inside the piece before overflowing into the container.

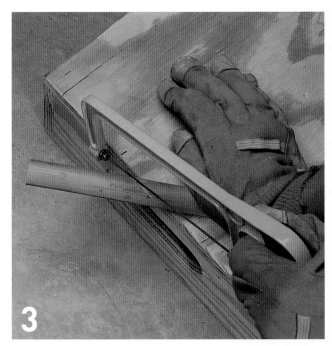

3 Angle Bamboo With a Saw
Cut the lip angles with a sharp saw. A hacksaw is one option. Once you've determined which end is up for each bamboo piece, mark off where to cut the angle. (Use photo to determine the angle of the cut.) Using a sharp saw will minimize shredding of the bamboo fibers as you near the end of the cut. The bamboo will be in contact with water. Some people like to waterseal bamboo to prevent dark discoloration and shredding that occurs after ten to twelve months of constant use. If you wish to seal the bamboo, you can use melted wax, marine varnish, polyurethane spray or liquid, or carnauba wax inside and out.

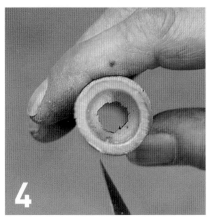

4 Cut Open the Growth Ring
With a craft knife or other sharp instrument, puncture a hole in the tallest bamboo piece, making a hollow pipe. Enlarge the hole to about ½" (13mm) so water doesn't shoot out under the increased pressure of a small hole.

5 Fit the Tall Piece Over the Pump Spout
Fit the hollow bamboo piece (pipe) over the pump spout. If it does not fit snugly, use a short piece of ⅜" (10mm) tubing, ⅝" (16mm) tubing or ⅞" (22mm) tubing to fill in the space. Telescope the tubing back down to fit over the pump spout. Or with an underwater glue, glue a piece of tubing into the bamboo pipe to make a tight fit.

6 Put Bamboo and Rocks in Bowl
Put stones in the bottom of the bowl, with larger ones on the bottom and smaller ones on top. Fill the bowl with water and plug in the pump to see how the water flows out the hollow bamboo pipe. If the pipe isn't straight, support it by adding pebbles around its base. Hold the other two shorter bamboo pieces against the central one to see what placement appeals to you. The taller angles should rest against the hollow bamboo so water will slide into the adjacent pieces on its way down the pipe. Move the pieces; for instance, one can face forward and the others can face toward the side. You can adjust them later if you don't like the water flow. Unplug the pump to finish assembling the fountain.

7 Bind the Bamboo Pieces Together

Secure the bamboo pieces with a rubber band to hold them in place. Tie with raffia, ribbon or string and hide the knot in back. Plug in the pump again. How does the water flow sound? Is it splashing out the bamboo pieces? Is the water missing the bamboo pieces altogether? You can adjust the water flow regulator to increase or decrease the water volume. The goal is to see water rising out the bamboo pipe, falling into the two side pieces, bubbling up out of them and falling into the basin. Add live bamboo shoots to the fountain by slipping the root end into the pebbles about an inch. They will continue their root and leaf growth in the fountain water with diffused light and room temperatures. The pebbles will keep the shoots propped upright.

8 Add Stones

Use a stone to cover the cord at the edge of the bowl. Add a touch of color with turquoise rocks or your favorite crystals.

9 Add a Plant

Slide a leafy green plant next to the side of the bowl to further disguise the cord.

As a meditation aid or center of a
home altar, your personal fountain
represents your connection to the
natural world and the essence of life.

materials

- submersible pump with spout that fits ½" (12mm) o.d. tubing, with water regulator set on low
- 1" (2.5cm) of ½" (12mm) o.d. flexible plastic tubing
- 1" (2.5cm) of ⅜" (10mm) o.d. flexible plastic tubing
- bowl at least 8" (20.3cm) in diameter and 3" (7.6cm) deep
- 6" (15.2cm) ceramic tile in color of your choice
- 4" (10.2cm) ceramic tile
- 2" (5.1cm) ceramic tile
- stones
- pebbles
- luster gems
- terra-cotta sealant (optional)
- spray bottle of water
- plywood
- masking or electrical tape
- variable-speed electric drill with a ⅜" (10mm) ceramic tile bit
- clamp

Thin, square ceramic tiles from hardware and flooring stores make ideal fountain pieces because they come in a

drilled tile fountain

variety of solid colors and decorative designs. The glazed clay is easy to drill with a ceramic tile bit in your electric drill. You can drill the holes in the center or off center as shown in this project; another variation is to use a square or rectangular bowl instead of the round bowl shown here.

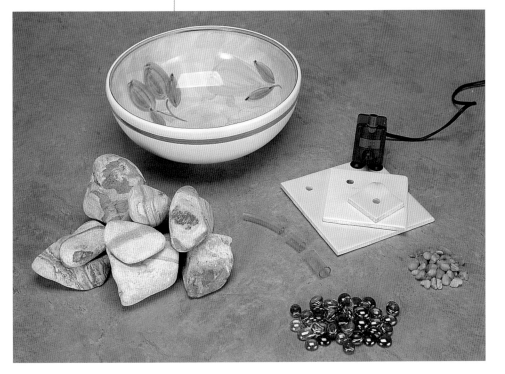

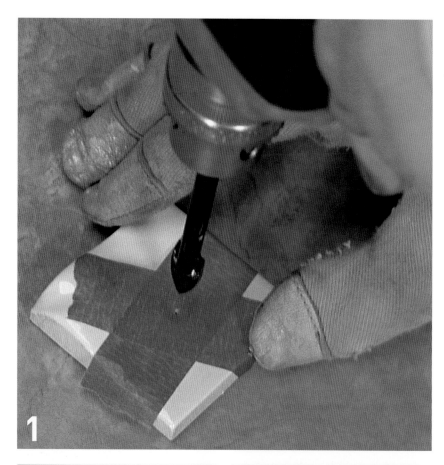

1 Drill Smallest Tile

Stack your tiles in various ways to determine where you want to drill the holes. Put masking or electrical tape over the approximate center of the tile. Draw pencil lines to connect the corners so you have an X in the center where the hole will be. The tape will prevent the bit from sliding across the glazed surface. As with drilling slate, clamp the tile to hold it in place and slowly drill straight down. Place plywood beneath the tile when drilling. Guide the bit rather than pushing it. Let the bit do the work. Spray the tile with water as you go to minimize dust and to keep the drill bit cool.

2 Line Up Tiles

Hold the first drilled tile at the corner of the next larger size tile. With a pencil through the hole, make an O to indicate the place for the next hole to be drilled.

3 Drill Other Two Tiles

Continue drilling the next two tiles with the hole in the corner, 1" (2.5cm) from the sides.

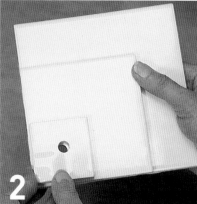

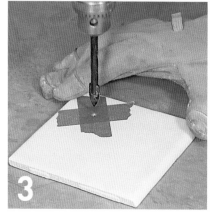

4 Seal the Tiles

The holes should be clean and uniform so the tiles will line up properly. You may want to protect the tiles from the damaging effects of long-term water exposure. Water will seep into the unsealed clay undersides of the tiles and eventually cause cracks and weakness. Paint water sealant on the backs of the tiles and let them dry.

5 Set the Pump, Add Tubing and Water

Put the pump in the bowl, off to one side so there will be room for the water to flow forward. (If you've drilled your holes in the center of each tile, put the pump in the middle.)

Cut about 1" (2.5cm) of ½" (12mm) flexible plastic tubing and fit it over the pump spout. Cut another inch of ⅜" (10mm) o.d. tubing and fit it just inside the larger tubing. The holes in the tiles are ⅜" in diameter and will fit over this smaller tubing. Add water and plug in the pump. Add a few stones around the pump to support the largest tile and keep it level. Unplug the pump.

6 Stack the Tiles

Thread the largest drilled tile over the tubing. Put three or four pebbles on the large tile near the drilled hole. These will act as spacers to elevate the tile layers and show more of the water falling. Stack the other two tiles the same way.

7 Stabilize Tiles
Slide stones underneath the bottom tile for balance and stability.

8 Add Accents
Add luster gems for color and sparkle. You could choose your gems to complement the colors in the room where you will be placing the fountain. The luster gems seem to belong with the smooth white tiles.

9 Adjust Tiles
Level the tiles so water pours off the tiles in an allover pattern, or tilt them for a more directed water flow.

The sound of rippling water has a natural calming effect that soothes the spirit and frees the mind from stress. The contemporary look of this fountain makes it perfect for a formal setting, such as a living room or office. On the other hand, the tiles may suggest to you that it would be more at home in the kitchen or even the bathroom!

- submersible pump with water regulator set on high
- 1" (2.5cm) flexible plastic tubing to fit your pump spout
- an old wok coated with a thin coat of vegetable oil or concrete and masonry sealant
- fountain fogger (optional)
- 3 pieces of drilled (⅝" or 16mm holes) slate, small, medium and large
- small slate pieces and flat rocks
- small stones (optional)
- ivy plant or other plant cutting that will root in water

Flowing water has a musical murmur that soothes the senses on a deep level, even when we're not consciously aware of its sound. Just looking at the contemplative setting of your handcrafted fountain will have a calming

zen fountain in wok

effect. Relax and soothe your senses with a slate fountain set in a seventies wok!

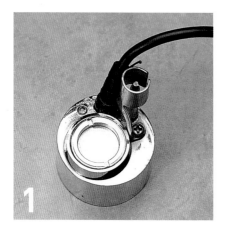

1 Oil Wok

Dig out that old wok and coat it lightly with vegetable oil (or paint with concrete and masonry sealant) to form a barrier between the metal and water. You might like the natural rusted look, but flakes of iron ore will eventually inhibit the ionizing fogger. (Or you can go with the rust and leave the fogger out.) For maximum water flow, set the pump regulator on high. Look over your fogger, read the directions and connect the cord with the transformer.

2 Set Up Pump

Set the pump toward the back of the wok and slip the tubing onto the pump spout. Add enough water to cover the intake valve, and plug it in to see how forcefully the water comes out. You may want to reduce the pressure later. Unplug the pump.

3 Stack Slate Onto Tubing

Drill your slate according to the directions on page 21. Scrub the drilled slate to remove grit, and stack the pieces onto the tubing, starting with the largest piece first. Plug in the pump again.

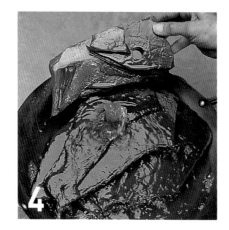

4 Adjust Slate Pieces

Shift the slate pieces around until you find a water flow pattern you like. You can separate the slate layers with small stones to emphasize the falling water.

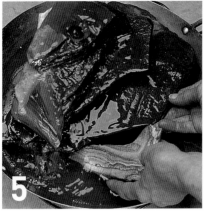

5 Add Stones

Now begin to fill the bottom of the wok with stones. A flat rock such as slate or sandstone will make a stable surface for the fogger to rest on. Here there is a second flat rock under the slate stack so the fogger will be between 1" (2.5cm) and 4" (10.2cm) under water. Deeper than 4" and the fogger's ionizer won't work. Less than 1" and the ionizer won't get enough water to work. Also, the fogger needs clean, debris-free water to work, so scrub those rocks!

6 Position Fogger

Plug in the fogger and slide it around to see where you get the best mist. Be sure it is on a flat rock and is under the correct depth of water. Leave about 2½" (6.4cm) of open space above the fogger.

7 Add More Slate

Continue adding slate pieces around the edge of the wok to fill in gaps.

8 Adjust the Amount of Fog

You can control the poofs of fog somewhat by putting the fogger partially under a slate ledge or by adding a piece of slate to partially cover the fogger. Leave some open space above the fogger.

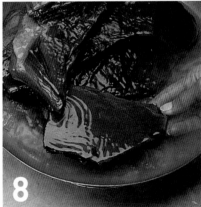

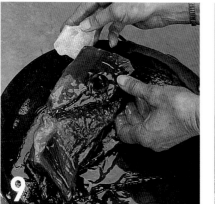

9 & 10 Direct the Water Flow

To get a concentrated water flow over the drilled slate, put a small stone under the back of the top piece of slate. This will direct the water forward so it doesn't flow evenly across the top piece but tumbles toward the center of the wok.

11 Add Plants

To hide the cord, add ivy leaves or a few sprigs of a plant that can root in water. Add these to the area where the cord leaves the bowl.

Voila! Your fountain is complete. This fountain would be a clever addition to your kitchen. It would also look wonderful on a patio nestled among potted plants or in a place of quiet in your home.

top ten fountain Feng Shui cures

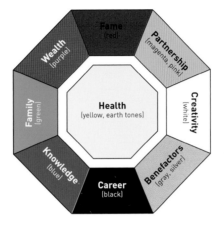

1. *Electrically powered objects.* An electrically powered fountain pump is said to promote wealth, a belief born in times when water was essential to the Chinese economy for its role in the growth of rice.

2. *Moving objects.* Flowing water and the moving air produced by the water currents capture the essence of Feng Shui ("wind-water"). Active *chi* and the creative forces of nature found in a fountain encourage abundance.

3. *Living objects.* Plants and flowers symbolize life and growth. In a fountain they breathe new energy into an interior and help circulate what is already there.

4. *Sound.* The rippling sound of moving water excites curiosity, pulling people to the source for a sensory treat of sight and sound. A fountain with wind chimes or bells will lure in *chi* (and customers) because of the unexpected sounds of wind and water.

5. *Heavy objects.* Heavy stones and statues in the fountain bowl restrain positive *chi* and keep it from leaving a space, enhancing health and emotional well-being.

6. *Bright objects.* Crystal balls, candles and mirrors brighten any interior and attract positive energy. A fountain with underwater light placed in the fame area draws life, happiness and positive regard.

7. *Colors.* Red, symbolizing happiness and strength, is the most auspicious color. Related colors, such as purple, pink and plum, are also fortunate. Green and blue-green promote growth and tranquility. Your fountain might have a red bird, rose quartz and green plants to draw in harmony and happiness.

8. *Bamboo flutes.* Hung diagonally from the ceiling or wall, bamboo flutes symbolize growth, stability and safety. You might place a miniature flute diagonally on a rock or use a hollow bamboo tube through which water flows.

9. *Ribbons, fringes and fragrance.* This category is open to additional ways to increase the flow of positive energy. Fountain fragrance might be in the form of an incense cone on a shell, an aromatherapy container set among the fountain rocks or a scented candle.

10. *The Ba-Gua.* Set your fountain in the gua, or area, you wish to enhance. See illustration.

- submersible pump with spout that fits ⅝" (16mm) o.d. tubing, with water regulator set on high
- 5" (12.7cm) of ⅝" (16mm) o.d. flexible plastic tubing
- copper T-fitting
- tinted glass bowl
- luster gems and stained glass squares
- 6 or 7 "blue ice" or "green ice" chunks of glass from a landscape yard
- submersible light (optional) pictured on page 90

A mosaic is the process of making pictures or designs by inlaying small bits of colored stone, glass or tile in mortar or grout. Here you will use colored glass squares and triangles to add sparkling highlights to the fountain. Create a mosaic by gluing the colored glass pieces to the outside of the

glass mosaic fountain

glass bowl. Then light up your fountain from the inside with an underwater light that shines out through the stained glass and flowing water.

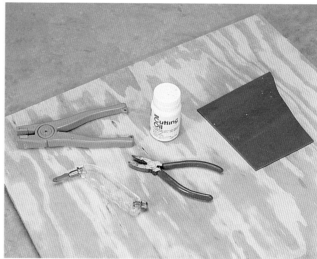

Materials to put a mosaic pattern
on the outside of the bowl
- 30 or 40 small squares and triangles of stained glass
- 20 luster gems
- E6000 glue
- small package of white grout
  (sanded or nonsanded)
- small package of colored grout to
  complement the color of your
  glass bowl
- tablespoon measure
- stirring stick for the grout
- cosmetic sponge, rag or palette
  knife to spread grout
- damp cloth
- paintbrush or toothpick

Tools to cut stained glass
- glass cutter with cutting oil
- glass nippers
- snub-nosed pliers
- remnants of different-colored
  glass, such as blue, green, red,
  pink and yellow
- work gloves
- ruler (optional)

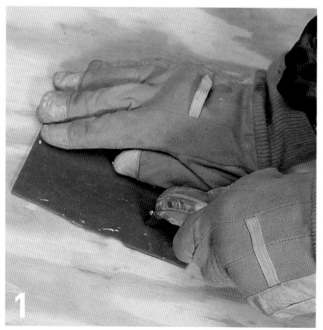

1 Cut the Stained Glass

If you haven't cut stained glass,
consult a stained glass book
from the library or take a craft
class at an adult education center. If you need a reminder of the
steps, follow these illustrated directions.

Add a few drops of cutting oil
to the hollow handle of the glass
cutting tool so the blade will
score smoothly.

To cut a strip of glass, make
the score by pulling the tool toward you with sufficient pressure
to make that light screeching
noise. Score freehand, moving as
straight as possible, or score
using a ruler as a guide.

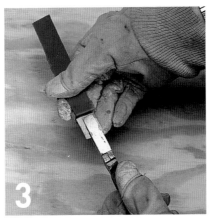

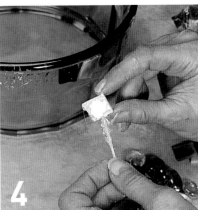

If you want to put a mosaic pattern on the outside of the glass bowl, follow steps 4 to 11. If not, go to step 12.

2 Break Off Strip

Use nippers to break the strip from the rest of the glass, lining up the ridge on the nippers with the faint score mark on the glass. Wear work gloves if you want to protect you hands from cuts.

3 Score and Cut Squares

Make one cut on the strip and break off the square with the snub-nosed pliers. Repeat along the strip, breaking off a square after each cut so the cut stays fresh and warm. These pieces can be put in your fountain for color, or you can use them as a mosaic decoration for the bowl.

4 Glue Glass Tiles to Bowl

Put glue on one side of about ten stained glass tiles at a time with a brush or toothpick. Let the glue begin to dry for about five minutes while you dab glue around the rim of the bowl. Letting the glue cure a little means the tile won't slip down when you stick it on.

5 Add Luster Gems and Let Dry

Gluing both the bowl and the tile ensures glue will cover the edges of the tile and grout won't slip under the edge. Set the tiles and luster gems about ¼" (6mm) apart for maximum glass exposure. Let the glue set for at least six hours.

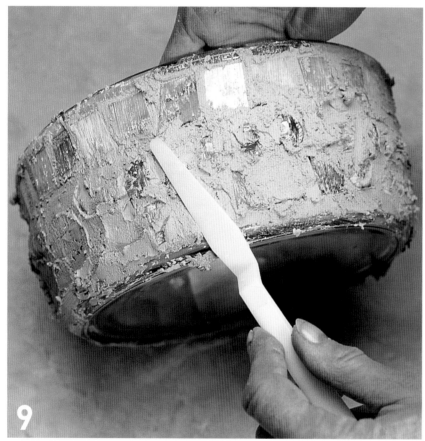

6 Mix a Test Sample of Grout

The grout formula for this mosaic fountain is four tablespoons of white non-sanded grout powder to one tablespoon of green sanded grout. Mix up a small sample of grout, spread it on some glass and let it dry to see what color it will be. Does it complement your bowl color? Add more color or more grout if it is not right.

7 Mix a Quantity of Grout

When you have a color formula that you like, prepare enough grout to cover the bowl. It is better to have some left over than to run short and have to mix a second batch that might not match exactly. Add a little water at a time, mixing after each addition until the grout is a consistent texture and spreadable, like fudge.

8 Grout the Bowl

Spread the grout over the tiles and luster gems, pressing grout into the spaces with a palette knife, rag or cosmetic sponge.

9 Smooth the Grout

A palette knife is a good tool for final smoothing of the grout. When you have a good coat of grout on the bowl, let it dry for about thirty minutes.

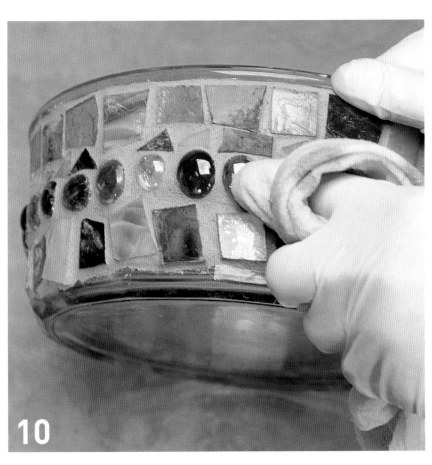

10

10 Clean Off Excess Grout

When the grout is dry, rub excess grout from the glass squares and luster gems with a damp cloth. Repeat three or four times until no more grout film remains on the tiles.

11 Put the T on the Pump

Start setting up the fountain. Twist the ⅝" (16mm) o.d. tubing into the copper T (it fits with a little persistence), and fit the tubing on the pump spout. The water will flow in two directions.

12 Put Pump in the Bowl

Put the pump in the bowl, add water and plug in the pump. If you are using the underwater light, put it on the bottom of the bowl near the pump.

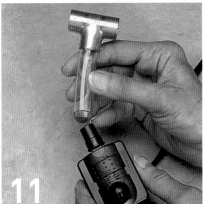

11

12

13 Add Ice Rocks

The tube with copper T may tip one way or another. Stabilize it by adding the ice rocks. Keep the rocks away from the top edge of the bowl so water doesn't travel along the rock and out of the bowl. Angle some chunks to catch the flow of water from the copper T.

14 Add Colored Glass

Scatter glass tiles over the tops of the rocks. Some will fall to the bottom of the bowl and add color there.

When you plug in the pump and turn on the light, the colored glass tiles on the outside of the bowl permit light to shine through. (This example shows the bowl without the mosaic.) The mosaic fountain enchants when the lights are dimmed to show the underwater light. This would be a romantic addition in a dining room for a candlelight dinner or in the living room to enjoy in the evenings. The beauty of the light shining through the glass combined with the soothing water sounds makes this fountain truly special.

personal supplies and reserves

Fountains and springs represent unending supplies and enduring reserves. In ancient Greece and Rome, springs were revered as the source of life and the origin of abundance constantly replenishing itself.

How are your reserves? Do you have the time and space to think about what you really want? How abundant is your supply of personal energy? Of money?

You can build a reserve by saving and investing. Another way is to remove anything that drains a reserve you already have.

Like water flowing in its proper channel, you may divert your resources away from people who eat into your reserves and supplies. Your fount of prosperity won't spring leaks when you reduce expense, eliminate unnecessary drains and build reserves.

perfecting your environment

What do you need in your surroundings to increase the quality, stability and order of your environment? For many it's a sense of feeling grounded. At work, for instance, a desktop fountain can be an oasis connecting you to nature. The sound of water rippling over stone is like white noise blanketing the hums and beeps of office machinery.

When you customize your environment at home or work, you may notice increased creativity. Improving or perfecting one aspect of your environment starts momentum building; and improving other aspects of your life becomes easier. For a self-check on life satisfaction in eight areas, visit www.springcoach.com/coach /index.html.

questions from "the coach"

I have been a certified professional coach since 1996. Coaching shares features with consulting and psychotherapy. Like consultants, coaches are often called in to address a business problem; unlike consultants who give advice, coaches seek solutions from the client to help the client move forward.

Like therapy, coaching is an ongoing relationship with an emphasis on listening, understanding and bringing internal obstacles to the surface. Unlike a therapist, a coach works with people who are happy with their lives in general and who are eager to move to a higher level of functioning, such as increasing joy, maximizing productivity or defining their life purposes. The process uses inquiry, support and accountability to increase the client's awareness and responsibility while creating a sense of balance and harmony in his or her life. Coaching is a bridge between desire and results.

A bubbling indoor fountain is one tool that you can use to harmonize your environment at home and at work. As a fountain builder, you may want to think about the qualities or values you are expressing in your home or office.

95

- submersible pump with water regulator set on low
- bowl at least 3" (7.6cm) deep (deeper than 3", use flexible plastic tubing on the pump spout to elevate the water)
- larger bowl or tray to frame the fountain bowl (optional)
- 12" (30.5cm) slate tile from hardware store broken to make three triangles
- florist's frog (in center of photo, there is a slate pin frog to hold flowers and water)
- cat or other figurine for decorative accent (optional)
- slate chips and pieces of decorative stones
- flowers (optional)
- fish bead
- toothpick
- white thread
- E6000 glue or clear silicone sealant
- E6000 glue or epoxy putty
- electrical or other tape
- rubber band

The focal point of this bubbling fountain is the fishing cat. You can use another figure, such as a turtle, frog or dragonfly, or leave out this accent completely. Water comes up from the drilled hole in the slate and flows over the ledge into the pool below.

slate ledge with cat fountain

The first step is to follow the techniques on page 20 to break and chip your slate square into three triangles, two that will stand up for the sides and one that will be drilled for the ledge. Before drilling the hole, decide if you want the water source close to the edge or farther back near the supports. Anywhere you want is fine. The hole should be ⅝" (16mm).

1 Tape Holes
The bowl for this project is a ceramic bonsai container from Japan. To fill the drainage holes, place blue electrician's tape in an X over the holes. Electrician's tape peels off easily when the putty is dry.

2 Plug the Hole
Turn the bowl over and fill the depressions with E6000, an underwater glue, or with epoxy putty. Either one forms a watertight seal.

3 Elevate With Larger Bowl
One option is to use a larger bowl to elevate your fountain container for greater visual appeal. This bowl does not need to have its holes plugged because it will not be containing water.

4 Position the Pump
Place the pump in the fountain bowl with the spout in a corner. Set the water regulator on low to start.

5 Fit Slate Ledge Over the Pump
The bowl is just the right height so the drilled slate fits over the pump spout and is also level with the bowl rim. The pump spout is ⅜" (10mm) diameter and the hole is ⅝"(16mm) diameter. The larger hole won't affect the water flow, but you could fit a very short ⅝" diameter piece of tubing over the pump spout so the drilled piece fits snugly.

6 Glue Slate Triangles
Put the three slate pieces together to form the ledge and backdrop. Determine which sides of the triangles you want to face in toward the fountain. Using E6000 or a clear silicone sealant, glue the backdrop together with one slate edge on the face of the other. You can glue the drilled triangle to the base or not. In this project the backdrop rests on the edge of the bowl and the ledge is on the pump spout, just level with the backdrop.

7 Add Stones and Water
Fill the bowl with slate pieces left over from breaking the tile and other stones. Add water and plug in. Adjust the loose slate pieces so they catch the water currents. To vary the sight and sound, set the water regulator on medium or high.

8 Add Accents

Add flowers, statues or decorative stones to the tray beneath the fountain bowl. The little cat with loose arms and legs is a Christmas tree ornament from Cost Plus. You can make a little fishing pole from a toothpick and a little fish bead, tied with white thread. The fishing pole and fish here were borrowed from a small clay Oriental fisherman. Put E6000 on the cat's paws, clasp the fishing pole between them and secure with a rubber band until the glue dries. Cut away the rubber band and you have a cat with fishing pole!

The foreground with flowers in a slate pin frog and multicolored rocks in the tray set the stage for the tumbling water in the background. This fountain would be at home on the hearth in a family room, on a patio surrounded by plants or on a hallway table.

how to quiet noisy pumps

- Buy a pump with a ceramic shaft that absorbs water vibrations, such as the Hagen Aqua Pump 1, shown here.

- Cut a sponge to size and use a rubber band to attach it to the bottom of the pump. This helps to absorb vibrations.

- Rest the pump on florist's foam or a rubber jar lid.

- Put bubble wrap under the pump, secured with a rubber band.

- Be sure that the pump isn't touching the sides of the fountain bowl.

easy ways to turn your fountain on & off

- Plug the pump into a wall switch and turn it on from the wall.

- Plug the pump into a timer so it will turn on and off automatically.

- Wire a timer into the wall socket.

- Use a remote control device, such as a garage door opener, to start or stop the pump.

- Plug the pump into an extension cord that has an on-off switch, which you place on a table nearby.

- Use a low-voltage pump with a transformer that has an on-off switch.

- Install "The Clapper" device to clap on and clap off.

- submersible pump with water regulator set on low
- 1" (2.5cm) of flexible plastic tubing to fit your pump spout
- 1" (2.5cm) of ½" (13mm) o.d. flexible plastic tubing
- 1" (2.5cm) of ⅜" (10mm) o.d. flexible plastic tubing
- 5' (1.5m) coil of ⅜" (10mm) o.d. copper refrigerator tubing
- large terra-cotta saucer, about 20" (50.8cm) diameter
- large terra-cotta pot (optional)
- sheet of ¹/₁₀₀" copper (.25mm thick)
- paper pattern for leaves from page 109
- 3 rainbow rocks or other easy-to-drill rock such as thin slate, or 1 rainbow rock and 2 pieces of florist foam
- rainbow rocks, sandstone or slate
- plant
- terra-cotta sealant, concrete and masonry sealant, or polyurethane
- soldering iron, paste flux, solder and sandpaper; or E6000 underwater glue or epoxy putty, and silicone caulk
- clear lacquer spray (optional)
- paintbrush or paper towel
- work or latex gloves
- salted lemon (optional)
- rotary tool with 2 cutting blades
- variable-speed electric drill with ⅜" (10mm) drill bit
- craft scissors
- clamp or vise

Reddish-brown, shiny, malleable copper makes a striking fountain. The sounds created by the water falling on the

copper leaf fountain

metal is melodic. You can clean copper with lemon juice and salt or let it develop a green patina as it is exposed to air and water.

1 Seal the Bowl

Start by sealing the terra-cotta (unglazed clay) saucer so it won't leak water. Wear latex gloves. Pour about three tablespoons of sealant into the saucer and spread it around with a paintbrush or paper towel. Add more sealant to well cover the inside of the container. For extra protection, seal the outside and bottom of the bowl as well. Or spray three or four coats of polyurethane spray inside and outside.

2 Put Tubing on the Pump

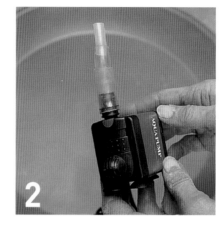

Assemble the pump and tubing with the narrowest tubing last. This ⅜" (10mm) o.d. tubing will fit part way inside the drilled rainbow stone. This drilled stone stabilizes the fountain base and holds the copper tubing upright. The ⅜" copper refrigerator tubing will fit in the other end of the rainbow rock and carry water to the top of the leaf. Set the water pressure on low. Water will be compressed into the narrow copper tubing, gaining pressure and producing adequate water flow.

3 Trace Leaf Pattern

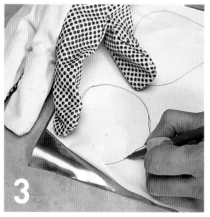

Pressing with your pencil, trace the leaf pattern from page 109 onto the soft copper sheet.

4 Cut Out Copper Leaves

A leaf indentation will remain and you can cut the copper with sharp scissors. The tallest leaf is somewhat long and narrow and the bottom leaf is shorter and wider.

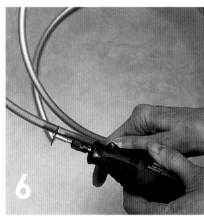

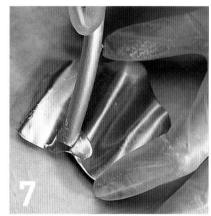

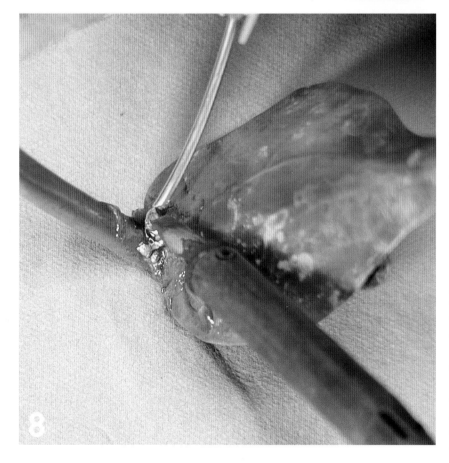

5 Bend the Leaves

Gently bend the leaf along a center vein, either straight or with a slight curve. Water will flow along this depression. To ensure water stays on the leaf, you can also bend the leaf edges slightly upward.

6 Cut Copper Tubing

Pull one end of copper tubing away from the coil and straighten it slightly using two gloved thumbs together, bending a little at a time, as shown on page 11. Cut a 10" to 12" (25.4 to 30.5cm) piece from the coil with a rotary tool fitted with two cutting blades. Because the blades are brittle and can snap easily if held at the wrong angle, use two blades for reinforcement. Cut another length of copper about 8" (20.3cm) long and a third length about 5" (12.7cm) long.

7 Glue Leaves to the Tubing

The long leaf will go on the 12" (30.5cm) tubing, the middle leaf will go on the 8" (20.3cm) tubing, and the wide leaf will go on the 5" (12.7cm) tubing. Use E6000 or epoxy putty to attach the stem to the underside of the leaf near the notch. Brace or clamp the glued piece and let it dry. Because copper tends to expand and contract with different temperatures, cover the dried E6000 with a silicone caulk.

8 Or Solder the Leaves to the Tubing

You could solder the leaves instead. Practice soldering with the smallest leaf and stem. The trick to soldering copper is to first clean the copper, then scar it up with sandpaper. Use a paste flux on the area to solder. Heat the copper with the soldering iron, not the solder. When the copper is hot enough, touch the area with the solder and the heat will draw it into the joints.

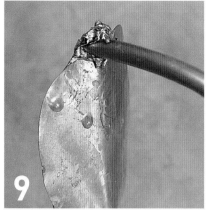

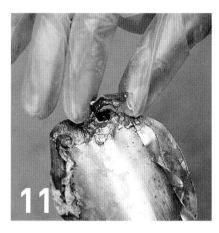

9 Sand Off Excess Solder

You don't need much solder to join the pieces. Using too much solder is a common mistake when learning to solder. The excess can be sanded off. When you have soldered the shortest stem to the wide leaf, solder the middle leaf to the 8" (20.3cm) stem.

10 Get Help in Holding Pieces

The hardest part is positioning the work in a vise or clamp so your hands are free to use the hot iron and solder. Ask a friend to hold the leaf and stem for you while you solder. Make sure both of you are wearing gloves because copper conducts electricity and heat.

11 Add a Cap to the Tall Stemmed Leaf

Position the copper tube about ¼" (6mm) above the notch of the leaf when you solder the tallest stem to the long narrow leaf. Water will be pumped up the tube and fall forward onto the leaf. Cut a little cap from the copper scraps about ¾" (19mm) long and ¾" wide to attach over the stem so water sprays onto the leaf and so the water source will be hidden. Attach with glue or solder.

12 Add Decorations to Leaves

For decoration, solder or glue some twisted copper scraps to the edges of the leaves.

13 Clean the Copper

Sprinkle salt on half a lemon to rub on the copper to clean it after soldering. If you want the copper to stay untarnished, spray the leaves and stems with several coats of clear lacquer.

14 Drill the Rainbow Rocks

With a ⅜" (10mm) drill bit, drill through one rainbow rock and part way through two other rainbow rocks. For safety, clamp the stones before drilling.

15 Set Stems in Rocks

Put the tallest stem into the rock that was drilled all the way through. Put the other two stems in the partially drilled rocks.

16 Or Set Stems in Foam

Or you can put the two smaller leaves in florist foam blocks. Don't put the tallest stem in a foam block because the foam will pack the tube and prevent water from flowing upward.

 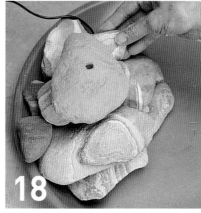 

17 Put Rock Over Spout

Fit the drilled rainbow rock over the the pump spout's tubing. (The copper stem was removed for the photograph, but this is the rock and tallest stem that you assembled in step 15.)

18 Add Stones

Slide supporting rocks under the drilled rock and next to the pump to build up the area around the tallest leaf and stem.

19 Add Water and Decorations

Set the bowl on an inverted clay pot to elevate the fountain if you like. Add the second and third leaves on their bases to the fountain, arranging them in a semicircle. Add water, plug in the pump, and see how the water flows. Shift the leaves and rocks around to get the sound and look you want. Add a plant and some copper scraps to the bowl for added color.

This fountain would make a dramatic addition to an entry. According to Feng Shui principles, a fountain by a door or entryway draws in career success and prosperity. That's the reason you may notice aquariums or other water features by the front door of Chinese restaurants. A large entryway fountain could be built in a marble trough or set on a wrought iron stand or inverted clay pot to elevate it.

The copper leaf fountain would also be appropriate for a patio or covered porch. If you put a fountain outdoors, use a pump that has a three-prong electrical plug so it is properly grounded.

- submersible pump with water regulator set on medium
- 6" (15.2cm) of flexible plastic tubing to fit your pump spout
- galvanized metal tub about 5½" (14cm) tall, 9" (22.9cm) wide and 16" (40.6cm) long
- brass watering can about 5½" (14cm) tall, 5" (12.7cm) diameter
- 18" (45.6cm) of 1½" (3.8cm) wide aluminum strip (depending on how high above the basin you want the can) with scattered precut holes
- 3 6-foot (7.2m) pieces of river cane or thin bamboo
- raffia strands
- floral foam
- butterfly
- rocks
- flowers, ivy
- E6000 glue
- 10 machine screws #10-32 x ⅜" (10mm)
- 5 machine screw nuts #10- 32
- 10 cut washers #10
- waxed paper
- marking pen and ruler
- latex gloves
- hacksaw
- variable-speed electric drill with ⅝" (16mm) masonry drill bit
- hammer
- awl
- screwdriver
- pliers
- craft shears or heavy-duty scissors

A watering can with its perforated nozzle sprinkles fresh flowers set against a reed fence. This colorful

watering can fountain

fountain garden provides a natural touch that beautifies any setting.

1 Cut and Glue the Bamboo

Because the glue takes an hour to dry, start with the fence. Make a garden fence from bamboo or river cane from a craft store or garden center. With a saw, cut lengths about 10" (25.4cm) long that will stick up about 8" (20.3cm) above the rim of the tub. Line them up on a piece of waxed paper and straighten the line with a ruler. Put on latex gloves and squeeze a strip of E6000 ½" (13mm) from the bottom. This will keep the canes together when you begin to weave raffia between the canes. Let the glue dry.

2 Weave the Raffia

For easier weaving, find the halfway mark on the raffia, weave in the lower half and then the upper half.

3 Finish Fence

One raffia strand is enough to keep the fence together; it doesn't need to be perfect because the flowers will cover most of the weaving. Tie or glue the raffia on the back of the fence. Set this aside to dry.

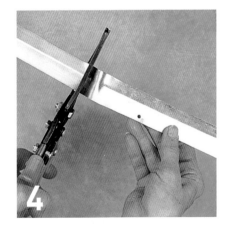

4 Cut Aluminum Strip

Next start on the support for the watering can. Select an end of the aluminum strip that has two holes precut. Measure about 12" (30.5cm) from that end and cut using craft shears or bend the strip back and forth along a fold to weaken the metal before cutting it. If your basin is deeper than 5½" (14cm), make that strip 13" to 15" (33 to 38.1cm).

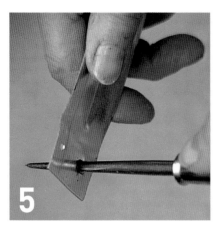

5 Make Holes for Screws
Make two holes in the aluminum strip large enough for the machine screws to slip through by twisting an awl through the existing holes.

6 Make the Third Hole
Place the strip inside the basin to determine where to make the third hole, which will support the strip at the top of the basin. Make the third hole to the left or right of the aluminum seam. You can make the hole by hammering the awl into and through the aluminum; put a piece of wood under the aluminum to catch the tip of the awl.

7 Mark the Basin
Make two more holes side by side at the other end of the aluminum strip. The watering can will be screwed to the strip here. Hold the aluminum strip inside the basin again, or hold the strip outside the basin and make marks on the basin where the three holes will go. Use a felt-tip pen or soft lead pencil. Make sure the marks are not on the basin's metal seam.

8 Make Hole in the Basin
Galvanized metal is easier than aluminum to hammer through with the awl, so go gently and make a hole that is just big enough for the nut to slip through.

9 Make Three Holes in the Basin

The two lower holes will anchor the aluminum strip, while the third near the top will brace it when it curves to support the watering can.

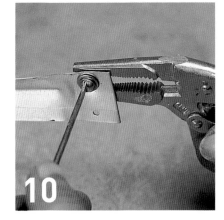

10 Lay Out the Parts

Now fasten the aluminum strip to the basin. Set out three sets of parts in this order: machine screw, washer (for the basin), washer (for the strip), nut. The washers have a flat side and a slightly curved side. The flat side goes flat against the basin to make a watertight seal. Use a screwdriver to tighten the machine screw and pliers or a wrench to hold the nut steady.

11 Attach the Strip to the Basin

Position the aluminum strip against the inside of the tub, fasten the two lower nuts and machine screws and slip the screw through the top (third) hole.

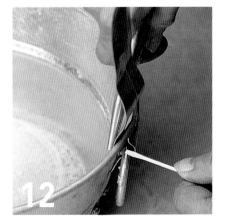

12 Tighten the Bolts

Remember to put washers on both sides of the hole. Tighten the screw. Sightly bend back the aluminum strip where it will support the watering can near the handle. The two holes at this far end of the strip will hold the machine screws going into the watering can.

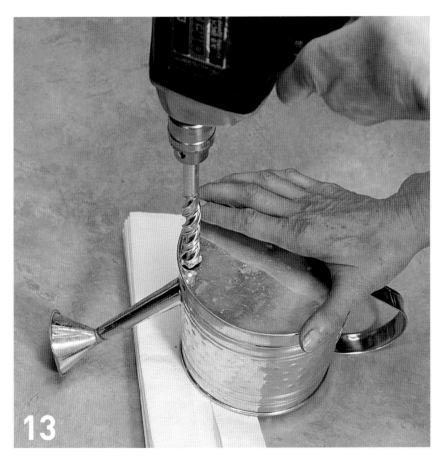

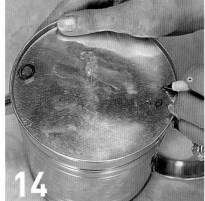

13 Drill the Watering Can

Prepare the watering can. Position the drill bit on the bottom of the can near the spout. Drill a hole with a ⅝" (16mm) masonry drill bit in an electric drill. The metal will resist and jump around, so hold it steady and drill slowly.

14 Mark the Strip

Put the watering can on top of the bent back aluminum strip and mark where the holes are to go as in step 7. Make sure you can easily see the marks.

15 Make a Hole in the Can

Bang the awl through the watering can to make the small hole.

16 Attach the Can to the Strip

Using the same technique of machine screw and washer on the outside, washer and nut on the inside, secure the watering can to the aluminum strip.

17 Connect Pump to Watering Can

Now let's see if all this hard work will pay off. The pump is under the watering can and the flexible tubing will connect the pump spout with the can. Thread the tubing through the hole on the underside of the watering can. The aluminum strip supports the can; adjust the angle of the can for the water flow you prefer.

18 Add Water, Rocks and Floral Foam

Fill the basin with water and plug in the pump. Sometimes the watering can's nozzle has holes that are too small and water will back up in the watering can, overflowing the top of the can. Reduce the water pressure if this happens or enlarge the holes with your trusty awl. Start decorating with floral foam on the bottom of the basin to hold the flower stems. Add rocks to fill in space and to support the reed or bamboo fence.

19 Add the Flowers

Stick short flowers into the foam in front. Add taller flowers in the background to lean against the fence. Add live or silk ivy around the tubing and aluminum strip.

20 Add the Fence

Lean the fence (above the water line) against the side of the basin, supported by rocks underneath. A butterfly atop the fence completes the garden scene.

This waterfall fountain enhances your decor and creates a tranquil environment. You could put the Watering Can fountain in a sunroom, atrium or kitchen.

top ten signs that you need "Fountains Anonymous"

1. Every flowerpot in the house is "missing," called into service as a fountain container.
2. You frequently shout to your spouse, "Stop the car, I see a rock!"
3. Your neighbor's landscaping is slowly (one rock at a time) becoming sparse.
4. You constantly find yourself saying (even in your sleep), "I can make a fountain out of that!"
5. You quit your job and join the St. Timothy the Potter monastery for a month or so.
6. You spend countless days in the garage breathing clouds of rock dust, wading in puddles of water and gluing your fingers together, all the while telling yourself, "This is fun!"
7. You become violent when someone responds to your fountains by saying, "It makes me want to pee."
8. You come to know the teenager who works the register at PETCO by his first and last name in your quest for the right rocks.
9. You convert every toilet in the house to a bidet.
10. You take all the straws from your kids' Chuck E. Cheese cups, just in case you run out of vinyl tubing.

Call "Fountains Anonymous" at 1-800-WET SHOES if you exhibit any of the above behavior.

Contributed by the tt-fountains@egroups discussion list.

117

a gallery of fountains

Use this gallery as inspiration for your own fountains. Most were created using the techniques in this book. Many craft stores carry fountain-building supplies; check Resources (pages 126-127) for hard-to-find items.

Feather Rock fountain with turquoise and aqua cove stone accents in round black bowl. Contributed by Elaine Nobriga of Ignacio, Colorado, this handcarved dark gray rock has water pools and rivulets to set a meditative mood and beautify any setting.

Experience a piece of the natural world with cream-colored Z-lite rocks bubbling over with flowing water. Driftwood, moss and the relaxing sound of flowing water create a sense of tranquility in your home or office.

A desert oasis splashes up in the center bowl surrounded by a flat slate ledge, oxidized green copper and bleached cactus spines. The hypnotically relaxing sound of water rushing over smooth stones clears your mind of the cares of the day.

This fountain was created using wooden vases that were treated like the bamboo pieces in the Bamboo fountain project. Two vases were cut into two unequal pieces. The tallest piece is completely hollow, and it contains the tubing attached to the pump. The shortest piece has the flat wooden bottom facing up. We sealed the bottom of one middle piece. It and the other piece fill up with water and spill over.

The Rotating Marble Ball fountain adds kinetic art to your home or office. This natural wonder of sound and motion is contributed by Glenn Harrison of Fountain Pumps, Inc. in Downey, California.

The Purple Heart and Oak Wood fountain brings beauty and elegance to small spaces. Cascading water sparkles as it dances downward over a drilled pagoda stone. Contributed by Glenn Harrison.

The Rose Quartz fountain with an underwater light is a magnificent sculpture of falling water and stone, a reminder of mother earth. Contributed by Glenn Harrison.

Black wooden bowl, tulips painted on rock, tumbling water and a bobbing glass oil lamp transform a home into a peaceful garden. Painted tulips contributed by Luba Semanisin of Rancho Bernardo, California.

The Purple Barnacle fountain overflows into a ruffled clam shell and falls into the pool below. Lower stress by listening to gently falling water as sea spirits grace your home.

The Lavender Rock fountain with a large amethyst tea candle holder and ceramic bowl from Target shows a lovely interplay of sight, sound and motion as water recirculates in tumbling cascades.

123

Modern art Blue Glass fountain is made of cups drilled with a ceramic-glass bit and filled with luster gems and an underwater light. Crushed velvet fountain cushion contributed by Susan Picklesimer of San Francisco, California.

The unusual finish on this gourd is a copper patina (see page 14). After the patina was created, the gourd was sealed for use as a fountain container. This fountain was created by photographer Christine Polomsky at F&W Publications.

resources

author's web site

Create Your Indoor Fountain!
P.O. Box 632864
San Diego, CA 92163
(800) 828-5967
Fax: (619) 280-7711
www.BuildFountains.com
Subscribe to Design on Tap, the free in-door fountain monthly e-zine!

general fountain supplies

Look in craft stores, such as Michaels and Hobby Lobby. Also check hardware stores, garden centers and aquarium stores. Or try these:

Artistic Delights
864 Los Positos Dr.
Milpitas, CA 95035
(408) 946-7972
www.artisticdelights.com

Cascade Dreams
5320 Roswell Rd. #C6
Atlanta, GA 30342
(404) 257-5912
www.cascadedreams.com

Fountain Builder
1841 CR 977
Ignacio, CO 81137
(970) 883-5346
www.fountainbuilder.com

Fountainheads
1827 Scott St.
San Francisco, CA 94115
(415) 921-7902

Neptune in Aquarius
P.O. Box 2486
Peter Stuyvesant Station
New York, NY 10009
(212) 460-5624
www.prosperityfountain.com

accents

Try gift stores or thrift stores, or use souvenirs you've collected. For other figurines, candles, shells, luster gems, incense, try these:

American Science and Surplus
3605 Howard St.
Skokie, IL 60076
(847) 982-0870
Fax: (800) 934-0722
www.sciplus.com

AzureGreen
P.O. Box 48-WEB
Middlefield, MA 01243-0048
(413) 623-2155
www.azuregreen.com

Dallas Bonsai Garden
P.O. Box 551087
Dallas, TX 75355
(800) 982-1223
www.dallasbonsai.com

Elaezar's Olive Oil Lamps
166 Commerce St.
P.O. Box 1384
Longview, WA 98632-7815
(800) 550-5267

Feng Shui Warehouse, Inc.
P.O. Box 6689
San Diego, CA 92166
(800) 399-1599
www.fengshuiwarehouse.com

Sanibel Seashell Industries
905 Fitzhugh St.
Sanibel, FL 33957
(941) 472-1603
Fax: (941) 395-1525
www.seashells.com

Shell Horizons
14191 Sixty-third Way
Clearwater, FL 33760
(727) 536-3333
Orders: (800) 330-2672
Fax: (727) 536-8888
www.shellhorizons.com

The Stained Glass Web-Mart
2808 Broadway
Eureka, CA 95501
(707) 443-8550
Orders: (888) 452-7796
www.glassmart.com

U.S. Shell
P.O. Box 1033
Hwy 100 and Madison St.
Port Isabel, TX 78578
(956) 943-1709
Fax: 956-943-6901
www.usshell.com

bamboo

Frank's Cane and Rush Supplies
252 Heil Ave.
Huntington Beach, CA 92647
(714) 847-0707
Fax: (714) 843-5645
www.franksupply.com

gourds

The Caning Shop
926 Gilman St.
Berkeley, CA 94710
(800) 544-3373
www.caning.com

bowls

Try department and discount stores, garden centers, pottery outlets, thrift and craft stores.

copper sheets

Copper sheets can be hard to find. Look in the Yellow Pages under Metals.

Handy Metal Mart
1540 McKinley Ave.
National City, CA 91950.
(619) 474-3379.

San Diego Hardware
840 Fifth Ave.
San Diego, CA 92101.
(619) 232-7123
www.sandiegohardware.com

fountain kits

For easy-to-assemble fountain kits, visit gift, book, department and craft stores. Also try these:

Mt. Woodson Waterworks
22947 San Vincente Blvd.
Ramona, CA 92065
(760) 788-7340
www.tablefountain.com
www.philly.cyberloft.com/mtwoodson

Wicklein's Water Gardens
P.O. Box 9780
Baldwin, MD 21013
(800) 382-6716
www.wickleinaquatics.com

plants

Check your local garden center for air plants and water plants. Or contact these merchants:

Black Jungle Terrarium Supply
P.O. Box 426
Turners Falls, MA 01376
(413) 863-4944
Orders: (800) 268-1813
www.blackjungle.com

Hughes Water Gardens
25289 SW Stafford Rd.
Tualatin, OR 97062
(503) 638-1709
Fax: (503) 638-9035
www.waterplant.com

Mother Nature's Gifts
P.O. Box 42-0340
Kissimmee, FL 34742-0340
Fax: (407) 935-1116
www.airplants.com

The Plant Stand
2972 Century Place
Costa Mesa, CA 92626
(714) 966-0797

Tropiflora
3530 Tallevast Rd.
Sarasota, FL 34243
(941) 351-2267
Orders: (800) 613-7520
Fax: (941) 351-6985
www.tropiflora.com

pumps (specialty)

Craft Warehouse
1355 NW 185th Ave.
Aloha, OR 97006
(503) 645-0603
(battery-operated pumps)

F&Q Pumps, Inc.
10617 Rush St.
South El Monte, CA 91733
(626) 455-0884
Fax: (626) 448-9462
(pumps and inexpensive rolling balls)

Real Goods
13771 S. Highway 101
Hopland, CA 95449
(800) 762-7325
www.realgoods.com
(solar-powered pumps)

rocks and stones

Landscape yards, garden centers, hardware store nurseries, beaches, forests and woods are good sources for rocks. For specialized stones, such as crystals, fossils, rock art, and agate slices, try these companies:

Coolrox Limited
P.O. Box 14591
Gainesville, FL 32604-2591
(352) 379-0440
Fax: (801) 838-6732
Voice mail: (888) 266-5769
www.coolrox.com

Feller Stone
688 E. Chad Ranch Rd.
Veyo, UT 84782
(435) 574-9300
Fax: (435) 574-9333
For catalog: (800) 776-2206
www.fellerstone.com

Nature's Emporium
900 Meridian E. #19-413
Milton, WA 98354
(253) 826-0510
www.natures-emporium.com

Signature Stones
1548 Burden Lake Rd.
Averill Park, NY 12018
(888) 795-6760
www.signaturestones.com

South Pacific Wholesale Co.
Route 2, P.O. Box 249
East Montpelier, VT 05651
(800) 338-2162
www.beading.com

rolling spheres

(also called Spinning Ball)
Kinetic Fountains
101 Brook St.
Black Mountain, NC 28711
(828) 669-1140
(800) 646-5658
Fax: (828) 669-1137
www.kineticfountains.com

Orbital Stone Works
2840-I Stirling Rd.
Hollywood, FL 33020
(888) 381-9214
Fax: (877) 952-2220
www.fountainology.com

index